A Thousand Miles of Mustangin'

A Thousand Miles of Mustangin'

BY BEN K. GREEN

Illustrated by Joe Beeler

NORTHLAND PRESS / FLAGSTAFF, ARIZONA

During *the late days* of the depression I had about used up all the hard ways to make a living ahorseback. I had bought and gathered outlaw cattle, broke and swapped and drifted horses and done whatever else I could do ahorseback. I guess there was foul and unpleasant ways of makin' a living afoot by hirin' out for wages, but I'd never done this and didn't see any sense to startin' now.

Since it was early fall and a cowboy should be figurin' how and where he was going to camp and what kind of a horse deal he was going to have through the winter, I decided to drift further west and look around in some new country for whatever kind of livestock deal that everybody else had played up or turned down.

My string of saddle horses didn't exactly suit me, but I knew if I ran on some stock work that might pay off, I could always get some more horses. I had a big stout bay horse that was past smooth mouth and I didn't really know how old he was but he could have been twelve to fifteen years. He was sound, and was also a good pack horse that I had bought for $27 in Fort Worth one day when the market was bad. Another one of my mounts was a good six-year-old strawberry roan horse, a little small, but he made up the difference with his know-how. Then I had a five-year-old light bay horse that was green-broke and still unpredictable but was good for lots of hard riding because I didn't have much sympathy for him. Last but not least, I had my old standby, Beauty, whose age wasn't hurtin' her much. It had seasoned her judgment some and she wasn't quite as reckless as she had been and was still by far the best horse I had ever had.

I left Weatherford early one Saturday morning with my pack on the old bay horse, riding the green-broke five-year-old, leading the strawberry roan, and Beauty grazed along the way and kept up with us. In a few days I had ridden into Abilene and made myself at home in Jenks McGee's Mule Barn. The country was extremely dry and it was a little early in the year for any horse and mule tradin' of a profitable nature. It seemed everybody's tradin' money had shrunk up. I was carryin' plenty of money to handle most any kind of a horse and mule tradin' deal for a quick turnover or if worse came to worst, I could winter myself without working and when a cowboy is in this kind of a financial fix, he don't have to take on something that don't suit him just to be makin' chuck for him and his horses. So I loafed around Abilene a few days and let my horses fill up and thought to myself that maybe I hadn't gotten far enough west.

In about a week I rode into Midland and didn't hurry through Sweetwater and Big Spring on the way, but there wasn't anything promisin' enough to interfere with my trip. I kept my horses in the railroad stockyards at Midland and fed them alfalfa hay a few days and loafed around the Scharbauer Hotel and heard a good deal of big conversation but didn't see any money changing hands and didn't hear of any kind of a cowboy deal that I could cut myself in on.

One afternoon in the hotel lobby conversation drifted to the Big Bend country and it seemed that they had a little more rain than the rest of West Texas and that it would be a good country to winter in. From the general conversation, it seemed that it was

2

a little too far for any of the natives to actually know much about it and most of what they knew was hearsay. Well, my favorite way of stopping hearsay was to go look! So I packed up my riggin' and took my mounts and started southwest to see what was in the Big Bend country.

It was early October, the weather was nice, the nights cool and the days warm and balmy — good kind of weather on both horses and men for travel. There was a fellow who was raised at Weatherford named Charley Green. He was no relation of mine and I had never seen him but I'd at one time leased the old Charley Green ranch at Weatherford that he had sold many years before. He was ranching in the Big Bend country and I thought I would make it to his headquarters and visit with him until I found out what he knew about the country.

I stayed in Fort Stockton two or three days and some of the cowboys there said that there were still some mustang horses in the mountains of the Big Bend country. Well, the horse business was pretty bad and about the only horse that would make any money would be one that wouldn't cost anything. I had been running the idea through my mind that maybe I could mustang a band of horses out of the Big Bend country by spring that would amount to winter wages at least and maybe more.

I rode into the town of Marathon late one afternoon and made camp and staked my horses out in a grassy flat on the south side of the highway and railroad next to an old mercantile building. I was in a big country that you could see way into day after tomorrow without anybody or anything being in your way. For the last week or two I had been riding in high rolling country that was in a drouth and stock were extremely scarce. However, coming from Fort Stockton to Marathon, I saw several bunches of antelope and deer were rather plentiful too. By the time I reached Marathon

I was in a real big wild country as compared to most of the ranch country that I had worked in.

Instead of setting up camp I decided I would pamper myself a little bit so I went over and got a room at the Gage Hotel after I had set up camp and took care of my horses. This was a good small brick hotel, well operated and only had a few people staying there. They served good grub and the conversation was light and enjoyable around the lobby. I talked to three or four people that night who were well acquainted with the country south of there described as the Big Bend country of Texas.

I learned that Charley Green's headquarters were in the Persimmon Gap region something like thirty-five or forty miles south of town. The next day I laid in as much grub as I could pack on one horse and bought a full-size slab of salt bacon. Salt bacon was far from being tasty to a cowboy that had been raised on good smoked meat, but it was about the only kind of meat that I could pack into the desert region that I didn't have to worry about spoiling. It would do to season beans and all other kinds of stuff that boiled with it, and, if it was parboiled, then battered and fried real good, if you was tough enough and hungry enough, you could eat some of it yourself. And just in case I did find a mustang or two, I bought a fair-size coil of three-quarter-inch stake rope and two Plymouth silk manila lariat ropes.

I left early one morning and that night camped at the Twin Windmills, an old landmark about thirty-five miles south of Marathon on the way to the bottom end of the Big Bend. This had been a narrow gravel road all day that was fenced and I had been told that the fence would run out somewhere during the second day's ride and that I should turn off to the east to go into the Charley Green ranch before the fence ran out. The Twin Windmills were in a location on Tornilla Creek where there had been natural

4

springs and when these springs had filled up, a pioneer rancher by the name of Miller dug the two wells and put up the two windmills around 1900 that were known far and wide and was the campground for all the early-day pioneers that freighted with ore wagons and who hauled wool and perhaps other contrabrand that came out of Old Mexico. This was also the stopover and watering place for herds of cattle on the way to the railroad.

Since I had laid in some fresh grub at Marathon, I fixed a big supper and I had bought a few bushels of oats that I packed on the roan horse so I fed my horses some oats and staked them out on some good grass for the night. Next day I rode into Charley Green's ranch about middle of the morning. He was at home and came out from around behind the house hollerin' "get down" and that kind of welcomin' stuff and I introduced myself and told him I was from Weatherford, Texas. This warmed the old boy up and we started a lot of conversation, mostly him asking about old friends and the changes that had been made in the country since he left. He finally looked at my horses and asked me where I was going. I told him that first I had come to see him and then I was going further down into the Big Bend.

He was sure glad to have me visit so I took my horses to the corral and piled my riggin' under a mesquite tree and went back to the house. He fixed us some batchin' dinner while we visited. By the time we ate up his grub, we had got real well acquainted and I got around to tellin' him that I had heard about some mustang horses in the Big Bend and thought I would go catch me a herd of 'em.

He said, "Now, Ben, I've been here a good many years and I've heard of those horses too, but I've never seen 'em and this is a big country. I don't think one man can ever catch any of 'em if he finds 'em. This is good winter country and you'd enjoy your stay. I'd be glad to have you so why don't you just winter here with me? Then when the grass puts out in the spring, drift on back into that lush old-time ranch country that I left and forget about this old hard world out here and them damn phantom mustang horses cause I ain't for sure that there's any atall in the Big Bend."

"Charley," I said, "that ain't gonna suit me. If for no other reason, I want to see the country and I want to know for sure that there ain't no mustang horses in here before I go back without any. I had it figured that I could probably catch enough by spring that they'd sell for what would amount to a winter's work. You've been off down here in this old world so long that you don't know that there ain't no place east and north of here to get a winter's work."

"Now, I ain't trying to run you off, but I had rather for you to winter here with me and go home with your horses still in good shape than to have you down in that old country south of here that I'm not for sure has got anything in it except a few stray Mexicans and rattlesnakes. I sure'd hate to have to write your folks that you starved to death or rolled down Christmas Mountain with a horse on you. That's about as near good as anything that's gonna happen to you if'n you try to spend the winter runnin' horses in this rough country."

Charley's argument and cookin' kept me around his place about a week. Then we rode into Marathon one day and spent the night. Next day we got on the train and went to Alpine just to see the country. Alpine was a pretty good size town of two or three thousand people and had a hotel, a picture show, several places to eat, Sul Ross College and a ranch supply store among other things. We caught a ride back to Marathon and Charley was ashowin' me how nice it was to be close to town. It was just a day's ride into Marathon and then if you wanted to go to Alpine, it was just

6

another thirty miles and it was awful handy. He explained to me that if I went deep into the Big Bend it would take me a week to get to town in case I wanted a piece of raisin pie. Of course, smart-like, I told him I would take a box of raisins with me and if I ran on to some good sound fat mustang horses that I could do without coming to town for a right smart more than a week. He kept up this kind of conversation all the way back to the ranch, but in a couple of days I loaded my pack and got my horses ready and started south into the big wild high country.

I was lookin' for horses all the time, but I was also lookin' for whatever else might be in there that I didn't know about. I stopped at Cooper's Store and camped one night. Cooper's Store was fifty or sixty miles from Marathon. I don't know how long Cooper's Store had been there but it was an old landmark and the people that ran it had a little post office or at least they got the mail for a few natives and kept a fair stock of dry staple groceries.

At Cooper's Store I followed the foothills of the Santiago Mountains south and east down to Dog Canyon where I went through Dog Canyon into a pretty good kind of high range grass country. Then still angling south and east towards the Black Gap Ranch, I camped at the headquarters of the old Black Gap Ranch which seemed abandoned and rode from the Black Gap around the mountains and over into Maravillas Canyon for several days. I packed up and left the Black Gap and rode toward the river and into Horse Canyon.

I had begun to wonder about the horses because I hadn't seen no sign of a horse and had run on to a goat herder with about three hundred angora goats that was camping close to a watering that was known as "The Hole in the Ground Tank." It was a man-dug well, but I have no idea when it was dug. I camped in an abandoned 'dobe house a few days where Stillwell Creek ran into the Rio Grande River at the old Stillwell Crossing, and the more country I rode out around one of these camps I made, the more I began to wonder whether there was actually any wild horses in the Big Bend and began thinking that Charley's story might be right.

I had a state highway map in my pack and began to look at it at night. It impressed me how little of the Big Bend that I had seen in the length of time I had been there and how long it was going to take to see the rest of it to where I'd ever know about the mustang horses that were supposed to be there.

I got all my camp together in my pack riggin' and crossed Telephone Canyon and began to follow the river and I came down to Boquillas Springs and there was a little old town across the river named Boquillas in the State of Coahuila, Mexico. I left my pack and extra horses in camp on the Texas side and rode into old Boquillas. It was sure nothing to brag about. However, I did get some Mexican grub and buy a few supplies at a commissary which is what the Mexicans call any little bitty country store.

I crossed back over the river next day and worked my way down to Hot Springs. This was a pretty fair settlement with a dozen people around it. I got to thinkin' maybe I was ridin' too close to the river to find any stock so I started working my way back up into the interior of the country again and made camp at Glen Springs for a few days. Whenever I found a white man or anybody else that could talk English, I asked them about the wild horses. They always told me that there was some in the Big Bend and most of them would always wind up tellin' me that they had never seen them but knew that they were in there.

It was an extremely mountainous old country with very few natural spring waterings and the canyon walls along the river were so steep that there were only a few places that stock could get to

8

the river to drink. I began to wonder about the springs and water holes and decided that I should be riding the spring holes for horses rather than just working the country in general. I rarely ever saw anybody between these small settlements and if I did, it would be some stray Mexican or half-breed Indian with a little *morral* which is a satchel-type pack that is carried over the shoulder and under the arm that holds his world's possessions, generally a few dried

tortillas and fried beans with maybe some sort of an old straight knife and sometimes a spool of thread for patching his clothes. When I found one of these fellows, he was always willing to be friendly hoping that I had some grub and they would pretty well tell me whatever I wanted to hear if they could find out what it was, and they would always tell me about the water holes and the wild horses were always over another mountain.

Up to now I still didn't have any mustang horses. However, I was running on to a good many herds of Mexican burros that of course were wild and unclaimed. That was easy to understand because they weren't worth anything in money and a Mexican needed only one or two of 'em to gentle and ride around on.

I continued to work on back up into the high mountainous country. As I got into the Christmas Mountain grass range, I saw some horse signs from there back down to Terlingua Creek where there were watering places and evidently there were horses either wild or being herded by somebody. I made camp high up on Little Christmas Mountain close to a little drip spring coming out of the wall of the canyon that would water me and my horses and perhaps a little game.

It had been more than a month since I had left Charley Green and I had just now begun to find some sign of wild horses. I used this spring for a headquarters and pretty well rode out Little Christmas Mountain and began to see where horses grazed. One afternoon about an hour before sunset, I rode up on a high mesa and looked down on a good band of solid-colored horses that from a distance I guess each one would have been about eight to nine hundred pounds and fourteen hands in height. The wind was against me and I carefully picked my way and got within counting distance of about twenty-seven to thirty head, not counting the colts that were with them. When they discovered me, they threw

10

their heads up and ran about a mile, then turned to watch me. As I rode in a wide circle around them, they made little signs of trying to get away and didn't appear to have ever been bothered by mustangers and their curiosity about my horse and me caused some of them to come out of the band and roll their noses and wave their manes and give me the once over.

I found these horses about the time that I should have been starting back to camp and I stayed with them till dark and rode back through the high country by guess direction and got into camp in the late part of the night. I chunked up a fire and cooked some venison from a deer I had killed and poured out a very small feed of oats for my horses since I was running short and went to bed thinkin' that I was about to catch some horses that had seen few people and few people had ever seen them.

I had been taking time about riding my horses and letting old Beauty rest most of the time, and by now I had a pretty good job of breakin' put on the young light bay horse. Since I might have a chance of getting a mustang today, I rode old Beauty and we left camp just after daylight. She was fresh and it was one of those brisk fall mornings and we moved on out from camp and covered ground pretty fast.

About middle of the morning I rode up on top of the same mesa and looked for horses and they hadn't made that part of their range that early in the day. This was all high country and I dropped down in some foothills and began to track this band of horses which wasn't hard to do. The grass wasn't too turfy and the terrain even though very rocky did show the print of a horse's hoof reasonably clear. About the time it was high noon I saw these horses shaded up in a small clump of live oak trees. They sighted me and didn't bust out of that shade real fast but started moving out suspiciously with the dry mares in front, then the mares and colts following and the stud working both sides and the drag keeping his herd together which meant that they intended to leave me for more peaceful territory.

Many stories have been written and picture shows have been made about wild mustang studs of all different colors, especially black, white and spotted ones, that seemed to have filled the imagination of the artists' souls that wrote such stuff, and in motion pictures, they always show the stud in front leading his band of mares. This is pure damn ignorance. A range stud never leads his band of mares. Usually the leaders are some of the younger mares that may not have foals at that particular time and then the mares with colts will be in the middle of the band of horses with whatever old mares or yearlings bringing up the tail and the stallion always rides herd from both sides and behind and points his leads by his own signals and protects the wings and the back of the herd. This is the way that this stud was moving his band of mares and I knew that there hadn't been any left behind or that had tried to leave the band.

I wasn't really quite ready to start a chase since I didn't know the range they were on too well and didn't intend to put them on too much notice that I intended to have a few of them, if not all of them, with my rope around their necks as early as possible so I reined back down the draw and rode the opposite direction and left them to wonder what I was up to.

I stopped when the sun was hitting the south side of a bluff. It wasn't too cold but was a nice kind of day in that mountain country. Beauty and I rested and we ate a little dinner that I had brought along wrapped up in my jacket with a small feeding of oats for her. I drifted back south and east around Turtle Willow Mountain and in the early part of the afternoon rode on to seven head of what appeared to be yearlings and two-year-old mustangs.

These would have been a part of the past year's colt crop that had been kicked off and weaned the winter before and had made the summer and fall away from the regular band of horses.

A stallion will cut out the younger members of his herd and kick and bite and drive them away to rustle for themselves until they are old enough to breed. The fillies develop first and will be picked up by older studs and the young studs will generally pick up fillies that are a year or so younger than them. This is one of nature's ways of keeping inbreeding from occurring in wild bands of horses. However, the fillies and the colts or studs will run together until they are coming two- and three-year-olds before they begin to split up.

It was easy to tell that these seven head had never seen a human being at close range or a man ahorseback and they made a wild dash with their tails up and heads out running at a stiff-legged pace until they were well out of danger to their inexperienced way of thinkin' before they stopped to see what it was all about. I knew that these would be the first mustang horses I would catch because they would be the easiest to outsmart and the slowest to outrun, but it was late in the day and I didn't dare to tie on to something that I couldn't get back to camp with.

The next morning I packed my camp and moved to the south side of Little Christmas Mountain at least half a day's ride closer to where these horses were ranging. This was pretty high country and sloped off to the south with plenty of open country and a few scattered trees out in front of where my camp would be where I could stake fresh caught horses. There was a small seep spring that would water a few saddle horses and a drip spring coming out of the cracks into a small basin that held about half a gallon of water that I could dip out of for myself. I set up camp on the south side of a big bluff on a little high green knoll that had formed from the bluff having caved off perhaps fifty years before and went to making plans to build some kind of a crude corral to keep my saddle horses in rather than to have them staked out where they might be at the mercy of a wild stud or some old fightin' mare.

Further up the canyon there were plenty of cedar trees. They weren't tall trees and I had to use some of the limbs for posts as well as the trunks. I worked the next three or four days cuttin' cedar and draggin' the posts and logs up against the bluff with a lariat rope tied to the saddle horn. I built two crude little corrals using the bluff for one side and got them high enough for any kind of broke horses, but I knew they weren't stout enough to hold very many outlaw horses that I might catch.

I had been lettin' my extra horses graze in the daytime and putting a horse in the corral at night. I had the old bay horse or the roan horse wearin' a bell when I turned them out so that they would be easy to find when I wanted to put one up at night. This is a good way to graze saddle horses. You should keep a good horse up at night to drive your other horses in with in the morning and from the horses that have been out all night, catch a fresh mount that is full and ready to ride. But by all means a cowboy ought to always have a night horse either in a corral or on a stake rope. Hobbling a night horse is a little too dangerous in that a hobbled horse can move his hobbled forefeet almost in the motion of a lope and get so far from camp that you are afoot — and then the hobbles sometimes come undone or break. A horse that has been taught to stake on a long stake rope can work the grass he is staked on in that circle and with experience, he will know how to keep from getting tangled up and rope burning his legs. A staked horse is usually as sure to be there in the morning as the strength of the log or tree or stake that you tie your loose end of rope.

14

The weather was always nice and balmy in the daytime — bright sunshine, no wind, always still and real cold at night. I intended to camp here a good while so I built me a lean-to close to the bluff as I could get it. I covered the top of the lean-to with cedar branches and some feed sacks to make it shed water. I needed to make myself a pretty snug bed so I took the finest of the twigs of the cedars and made a bed about a foot deep back under this lean-to and put my bedroll on that pile of cedar twigs and needles which softened up the ground considerably. I had plenty of blankets and a heavy duckin' cowboy bedsheet to make the winter.

After having taken off a few days for this building a new home, I started back riding and looking for wild horses. While I was doing all this hard work afoot, I got to thinking how much less those yearlings and two-year-olds would be worth than some of the big horses and told myself they would have to get in my way if I caught them first — that I needed to trap for something that would finally bring more money.

The first morning I rode out I found the stud with his band of mares and they seemed to know I was carryin' a long rope with a big loop because they moved on up into the high country ahead of me. I lost them for an hour or so and found them at a suckhole kind of a spring. It was clear water but not a whole lot of it in a flat in the middle of a draw along the head of Terlingua Creek. This water hole wasn't going to be much help from the standpoint of me being able to camouflage and wait for them because it was out in the open with no timber or canyonlike depressions around it.

I studied these horses pretty close and saw that there were only eleven colts on these mares. There were young mares that either hadn't bred or there was a strong possibility that some colts had been caught by panthers when they were small. I stood real still and watched these horses fill up on water and they stood around

15

the water hole a long time. When they left the water hole, they started up into higher country. I thought it might spoil 'em from now on, but I was gonna have to start running 'em sometime and had a good chance to run on to one of those better lookin' dry mares when she was full of water and goin' uphill before she could get to any brush to run in so I shook out a rope and gave old Beauty atalkin' to and we took out after this whole band of mustangs.

Now the ones that I had rather have were in the lead of the band. I circled a little bit and came in on to the side of 'em to where I would still be turning 'em uphill and some of the older mares with colts dropped back out of the way. I picked out a good blood bay mare and called on old Beauty for all she had and fitted a rope on that mare's neck right behind her ears where she would choke quick and wouldn't pull as much as when you caught her low down

on the neck. Old Beauty was used to jobbin' her feet in the ground and stoppin' everything I caught. I knew that wouldn't be the best because I would be taking the chance of breaking my rope or the rope cutting itself when that eight hundred and fifty pounds of horse hit the end of it. I spurred Beauty pretty deep and talked to her and got her to slow down and choke this mare to a stop instead of jobbin' her feet in the ground and tryin' to turn her a flip and bust her and knock the air out of her.

I always double half-hitched my lariat rope to my saddle horn. I never wrapped and dallied and gave slack when ropin' stock. That's the way to lose fingers in the rope and that's the way to get your hands rope burned and lose what you've caught, and damn a coward, if you haven't got nerve enough and confidence in your mount to double half-hitch and hard tie, you are going to scar up your hands and lose more stock than you keep.

Old Beauty took a firm stand and that mustang wasn't jarrin' her very much, and the mustang went to pullin' and kickin' a little in a circle trying to get loose from that lariat rope and the more she pulled, the more she choked. I had a hand-tied rope hackamore off my saddle and was on the ground waiting for her to fall. Pretty soon she lost all the air she had and fell to the ground. I spoke to Beauty to give her slack and rushed up to her head and shook the rope to where she could get her breath and before she could get to her feet, I slipped the hackamore on her and tied the throat latch. Then I took the long lead rope of the hackamore and hurried back to old Beauty.

I untied the lariat rope from my saddle horn but I didn't take it off the mustang. I dallied the hackamore rope where I could take up slack and when the mustang got to her feet, she was draggin' a lariat rope just in case she got away from me and I had the hackamore rope dallied with no more than six feet of slack between

18

her head and my saddle horn. When she got her breath, she came up pawin' and tryin' to run. When she was running the direction towards camp, we ran with her and when she tried to change direction, old Beauty would stop and I would put my hand behind my leg or behind the back of the saddle and pull her back around in place with the hackamore rope. This all happened pretty fast and it was all pretty rough, and it didn't take long for that old mustang to decide that she wouldn't move at all. When that happened, I rode around in a circle and jerked her forefeet off the ground where she would have to take a few steps and slowly get her to lead and drive on the way back to camp.

We weren't very far from camp and in about an hour and a half I had my first good bay mustang hard tied to a big stout, gentle cedar tree in the flat out in front of my camp. I had gotten a chance to see her mouth and teeth and she showed to be about a five-year-old with a good body, good feet and legs. This was the first day's work that had any payback to it since I left home in September.

I fixed a good batch of grub for supper and sat around the fire and watched this mustang mare try that stake rope until the night was pretty cold. She hadn't quit pullin' back and groanin' and tryin' to get loose when I crawled into my camp and went to sleep.

Next morning was a cold bright crisp morning and I layed in camp and let the sun get a head start before I crawled out. When I got my clothes on and walked over towards where I had staked my mustang mare, she was wadded up and lying on the ground. I kicked up the fire in camp and threw some fresh wood on the coals and thought while it was burning down where I could cook on it, I would see about my mustang. She had wrapped herself up in that forty-foot stout rope to where you could have shipped her parcel post and she wouldn't have got loose.

I knew better than to untie her head and me afoot, so I rolled her around over the ground and began to get her a little slack so that she could get her feet loose and get up off her side. I booed and boogered her until I got her legs and body unwrapped and she was standing without pulling on the hackamore rope. She had rope burned every leg and had her head pretty well swelled and skinned up from pulling on the hackamore and I said to myself that in another day or so she was going to take a little better outlook on being caught.

My saddle horses had stayed pretty close during the night and watched the excitement. I took the one horse I had in the corral and drove the rest of them up and decided I would ride the old bay horse and give Beauty a rest. I rode back to the Terlingua Creek country where I had found the horses the day before and they seemed to have changed range and I knew this would happen when I started running 'em.

About early afternoon I ran on to them over on Alamo Creek and when I rode up on them, they were around the side of a bluff and we surprised each other. However, the old bay had smelled them I guess and it didn't seem to be any surprise to him. It looked like maybe he was kind of smart on this horse catchin' business because he quick broke into a run. I shook out a rope and was about to catch a horse when we got into some rough rock country and I just had to check him up a little bit — my nerve failed me. As we came off this shaley rock place, it looked like he was a little aggravated at me for having pulled him up. He sure did break into a hard run and put me up next to a poor mare and she was the closest one to me and the only one that I was going to get a throw at.

I took my chances and made a bad throw. My rope went beside her head and the rope dropped back down along the side of her legs and sure enough I caught her by the forefeet. Well, ropin' the forefeet is a good way to catch horses if you've got some help, but catchin' a mustang by the forefeet by yourself is kind of rough stuff. Even though the old bay had jerked her down on the ground, he was having trouble dragging her enough to keep the rope tight. I got down on the ground with a hackamore to put on her head and the rope on her feet had a good chance of coming off if the old bay ever let her get any slack. This was the first time I had really tied to him and I found out I was sure enough ahorseback. He kept that rope tight until I could take a couple of wraps on her forelegs and I nearly knew when I untied 'em that she could get out of that lariat rope that was still on her but Old Bay was sure wise.

When you've got a horse on the ground, never walk up to their bottom because they can strike you with both hind feet and maybe their forefeet. You always work from over the horse's back by putting your knees on the withers and leaning over and reaching down from the back of the horse to the feet. This way there is little chance for them to be able to hit you with their legs.

I slipped back off of her withers and reached over and put my hackamore over her nose and pulled it up behind her ears and tied the throat latch real good. As I took the rope off that mare's legs, I spoke to Old Bay and he backed up real tight and took the slack out of the lariat rope. When I got the end of the hackamore rope off of her legs, I hurried right fast and got on Old Bay and got a good tie on my hackamore rope to my saddle horn. Then we moved up and gave her slack, the rope came off of her forelegs as she got up. While all this was happening, the rest of the horses ran off, but I could tell that the mustang mare had milk in her bag and one of those colts must be nearby. While she fought the rope and ran in a circle with Old Bay circling to keep from getting tangled up, I heard a colt snicker, and sure enough, a good brown colt had left the herd and come back to his mama. He talked in plaintive colt tones and she nickered and answered him and they had quite a carrying-on and he finally came right in close to her. I thought we had better give him a little time to make up his mind that this was Mama and he could suck if he wanted to and then he would follow us back to camp.

I had got my lariat rope up off the ground and had it done up on the other side of my saddle. I eased Old Bay up and took about twenty feet of slack out of the forty which left about twenty between him and the mare and we started to camp. This old mare wasn't too interested in leading and it was a pretty long trip, so between the distance and the fight we got in just a little before sundown. I still had plenty of daylight to stake her out and put my horse up and fix supper.

I noticed the first mustang had quit fighting her head and the rope and was awful sore and bad rope burned and had begun to eat some grass on the ground that she could reach and I expected by now was developing a fair amount of thirst. I kept Old Bay up that night and gave him just a little bit of feed because I was nearly out and used him the next morning to get up my saddle horses.

After I had my breakfast and got up the horses, I thought it was about time to tempt that first mare with a little water. I got a bucket and dipped it in the seep hole which was about a hundred yards away and carried it to her. She ran and turned herself a flip and got up with rollers in her nose and in spite of all the skinned places and bruises was still a unbroke mustang. I sat the bucket of water down where she could reach it from her stake rope if she decided to come that direction and stuck my hand in the bucket and splashed my hand in the water to give her an idea what it was. When she smelled it in the air, she eased up and stopped pulling on her sore head. I put the water about ten feet closer and she looked at it and snorted but wouldn't come closer. I noticed when I got about half way back to camp, she was up smelling of that bucket. I sat around in the distance and watched and it took her a good while to decide to drink out of that peculiar looking spring.

I eased back down to pick up the bucket and she ran to the far end of her rope, but she had sucked the water down to the bottom and that would be her earliest experience of somebody bringing her something. The first thing you can do to teach a mustang to pay you some mind is to let them get thirsty and then let

them know you brought them some water. Don't give them much the first day or two and they will finally get to where when they see you they will nicker and beg for something to drink. Of course, range horses have never been fed, and usually in a horse camp, you don't have feed to give 'em and you begin to hunt places where you can stake 'em and put 'em on fresh grass.

The next few days I found these horses just one more time and it was clear to me that it was likely that there weren't any more mustangs in the Big Bend except that one band of mares the stud was herding. The only chance I had had in the last few days of catching one was going through a narrow canyon and the stud was behind. I almost made the mistake of spillin' my rope on him when I realized that if I caught him, that bunch of mares would scatter and be even harder to track down and catch and I had better leave him to hold them together. By now they were pretty spooky and I thought maybe I ought to let them rest a few days before they quit the country and I had to hunt them some more.

As I rode into the edge of my camp late that afternoon, I noticed that the ground had been swept around the little rock fireplace that I had put together and a few things were hanging on the fence, like loose ropes and stuff. There was a pile of cut wood and broke about the right length. There was a fresh pot of beans boiling and the fire looked like it had been chunked up all afternoon. I knew that a stray Mexican had found my camp and was going to move in and camp with me — all of which would suit me for a while and if he wasn't a pretty good hand and a pretty good fellow, I would run him off.

As I looked around, I found him placing rocks in the seep spring to keep the water from muddying so bad. I hollered at him and he played like he hadn't seen me and I knew damn well he had. Then as he turned and walked up, I gave him the once over. He was a little fellow, weighed probably one hundred and forty pounds, past middle age with a straggly beard and a handmade cactus fiber hat on and those old white duckin' cotton clothes that are so common among the Mexicans and Indians along the border. He had a pair of *zapatas* on his feet that were made out of old automobile tires. This was another common piece of wear that they had learned to make from the fiber of old automobile tires. When they got through cutting them and putting straps on them to fit them on their feet, they were really a pretty good kind of footwear to protect their feet from rough rocky country.

He waved his hat around and grinned a big smile, still wondering whether I was going to visit with him or order him off and he went to telling me in mixed English and Mexican about cleaning up in camp and that he had put on some fresh beans. I asked him, "Wasn't there some fresh beans in the pot?"

He said, "Si, señor, but that was before I got here."

He had eaten up about a quart of beans and decided to earn his keep by cleaning up camp. When I stepped down on the ground, he reached over and got my bridle reins and led my horse to the corral and unsaddled him. Since I hadn't had any of this kind of spoilin' in a long time, this Mexican was makin' a hit with me. We visited and it was getting late. I said we ought to fix some supper and he said for me to show him what we would have and he would cook it — he didn't know where the rest of the grub was except for the frijoles. I had glanced at his feet and he had an old dried cut on his instep that had been freshly greased with salt meat rind and I said, "No, you don't know where the grub is. How come you to grease your foot with that salt bacon?"

He grinned and said, "Señor, you're pretty sharp."

We went over to the bluff where I found a crevice that would hold all my grub and be out of the weather and it wasn't likely that

varmints or other bugs would find it. I told him we would have some meat, which was salt pork, and some of his fresh beans for supper and he could make some flour tortillas. These drifting kind of Mexicans that roved around in the Big Bend and lived off the land through the winter seldom had anything but corn tortillas, and flour tortillas were a treat for them. He smiled big as he got ahold of a sack of flour and baking powder and I noticed him looking around among the rest of the stuff. He said, "I don't understand where the coffee is."

I told him, no coffee, that I didn't drink it. This was a great disappointment to him and he took on considerably about a cowboy that didn't drink coffee. By the time we finished supper it was dark and we had gotten pretty well acquainted and he had heated some water and washed the supper dishes. I asked him what he had to sleep on. He went over behind a rock and brought back his *morral* that had everything he owned in it and an old thick heavy hand-woven wool blanket. I told him to make his bed on the other side of the horse corral and if he didn't have enough cover, he could use the burlap feed sacks I had saved to put under his blanket. He was *mucho gracias* for all this and it looked like I had found me a pretty useful friend for as long as he would stay. It was a good cold desert night and I got a good night sleep and supposed Amigo did too.

Along about daylight, I peeped out from my duckin' bedsheet and saw that Amigo was putting fresh wood on the fire and getting ready to start the day. About that time I heard a roaring noise way in the distance and noticed that Amigo stood up straight and looked off to the north. I got up and pulled on my clothes and went over to the fire and every now and then, this noise would get louder. Well, there were no roads and I didn't think any place for one in the direction that I was hearing this roar. As it got closer, Amigo went to getting excited and said maybe so he ought to hide in the rocks. I told him it wouldn't make any difference — it wasn't after him. He said in Mexican that he wasn't thinking about whoever it was, it was whatever it was, meaning of course, he hadn't seen many automobiles in his lifetime.

Every now and then this noise would get louder and by sunup, three men drove up to our camp in an old-time high wheel pickup truck with a fifty-gallon gas tank in the bed of the pickup as well as the tank that was originally built on it. They killed the motor and got out. We shook hands and they told me who they were and Amigo had braved up and come from back of the corral. The first thing he asked was did they have any coffee. One of 'em said, "Damn right, and we're anxious to make a pot."

They got out a big granite coffee pot and some freshly ground bean coffee that was put up in a paper bag. After the coffee got to boiling and smelling good and they had warmed up by the fire, they got around to telling me what they were doing down there. They were from Kansas City and some smooth tongue promoter had sold them a section of land and furnished them a map with it for a hunting paradise. They had been lost for about three days trying to get around over that country in that old pickup ahuntin' their "lost paradise." I tried to explain to them that practically all the Big Bend was either state land or nonresidence ownership land and that practically none of it was fenced and that there were no survey points to go by and they might never find their lost paradise. This all seemed quite a shock to them and I was the first man that they had found that could talk English in the three days that they had been lost and they wondered where they were going to kill a deer if they couldn't find their land. And I said, "Hell, you better hunt the deer. You'll come nearer to findin' it than the land."

Amigo spoke up and said there was *mucho* deer up on top of

27

a mountain and he pointed to the southwest and told about it. There I stood between two foreign languages. Amigo's Mexican was easier to understand than the damn fellows from Kansas City. By this time, we were cookin' breakfast together. They were furnishing Amigo coffee and everybody was enjoying the morning as the sun began to come out and warm the sleepy old desert. For Amigo and three men from Kansas City to show up in one day and night was a right smart of excitement since I hadn't seen much of anybody for about six weeks.

The fellows were all rigged out with fancy store-bought hunting clothes, new rifles and enough ammunition to start a war and asked if they could camp there with me while they hunted deer. Of course most kinds of company was welcome, especially an outfit that was carrying canned goods, fresh smoked bacon and coffee for Amigo. Amigo gave all kinds of directions about these deer and I tried to translate them into Kansas City conversation. These three fellows were all pretty stout and in their late forties and fifties. They packed themselves with their guns and canteens and ammunition and started off towards the mountain where Amigo said the deer were.

After they were out of sight, I said, "Amigo, how do you know there is any deer on that damn mountain?"

He said, "Señor, Benito, what difference do it make? There are none in any direction."

I told him he ought to be ashamed and he said he guessed not. They would get their exercise and he could finish drinking up that last pot of coffee.

I stayed around camp that day and worked with the two mustang mares that I had staked out. The first mare I had caught wasn't exactly taking on civilized ways, but with a sore head and rope burns and me carrying her some water, she had gotten to the stage of trying to get along with me and wasn't too much trouble to lead to the spring to drink. The second mare that had the baby colt wasn't quite as willing but since she wasn't near as good a flesh, I didn't find her too much trouble to handle afoot and lead her to water.

I staked them both on fresh grass and this little colt kept staying with its mama. I thought it might be easy to ease around and throw a rope over her back when the colt was on the opposite side and catch it. I started to do this afoot and then I thought I'd better have a horse to tie that colt to so I saddled up Old Bay and eased around that mare with a rope and in a few minutes, the colt was

standing on the other side of the mare from me. Although I couldn't see it good, I could stand up in the stirrups and get a pretty good idea of where its head was so I spun a rope and pitched it over the mare and as the mare jumped one way, the colt jumped the other and went right into my rope. I wheeled Old Bay and dragged the colt out from the length of the mare's rope to where they wouldn't get tangled up together. The little fellow choked down pretty quick and I had already tied a hackamore in the end of some of that soft rope that I had brought from Marathon. Instead of tying this little fellow, I cut this rope off about six feet long and let him drag and step on it and let him graze near his mama and still be easy to get to her to suck.

This is all right with young colts because they step on the rope and pull their heads a little at a time and readily learn to give to the pull of the rope. It's just a matter of two or three days until you can catch ahold of the drag rope and lead them without ever being very brutal to them or knocking any hide off or rope burning their feet or legs.

This catching one horse at a time and maybe riding two or three days for each horse caught was going to use up a lot of time and a lot of horses and more than aplenty of me. Since I had some help, I was thinking about some way of running these horses by relays until they finally drove enough to try to drive 'em into my little corral. I knew this wouldn't be easy, but I knew too that I might manage to catch several horses at one time. I talked this over with Amigo and the more I talked to him and the more he talked to me, I realized he wasn't a horse Mexican and that he wouldn't make much of a hand at driving or catching mustangs.

He suggested two or three ways of setting rope traps around over the range that he just knew would catch horses. Range horses aren't too bad about going around hunting a rope trap to stick their

30

head in and I doubted seriously if what he was talking about would catch any. However, I had plenty of soft rope and we cut it into about thirty-foot lengths and made loops that would stand open four or five feet if they were swung to trees or rocks. He seemed to know the country pretty good and must have wintered in the Big Bend before. He told me about several of the trails where there were trees of sufficient size that the ropes could be strung on and the end of the rope could be tied to big enough trees to hold a horse. A lot of the brush in this country was small and scrawny and wouldn't do to tie a rope to that was going to get much pull on it.

I had an old saddle that I was using for a pack saddle that could be fixed up a little for Amigo to ride and I told him that we would get some kind of rawhide first chance we had and fix this old saddle up. He wasn't horseman enough for this to interest him and he said he would just as soon ride bareback with a blanket which is Indian style and not a bad way to travel if you're good enough rider bareback. I had an extra saddle blanket and we rigged up Old Bay. Amigo did a artful job of fitting these rope loops around Old Bay's neck down against his shoulder like a collar would fit and soon after dinner he rode out and said he would be back late that afternoon and tomorrow we would have *mucho* horses caught. Well, I knew that it wouldn't hurt to try and if he caught one it would be worth the trouble.

The group of Kansas City Daniel Boones come into camp about middle of the afternoon tired and give out but packing two small deer. They were delighted with their experience and thought very probably that the section of land they had bought for a hunter's paradise must be on top of that mountain. They discussed this around the fire half the night and it was sure all right with me for them to put their section wherever they wanted it.

Amigo came in about sundown and finished skinning and

31

dressing the two deer and cut off plenty of steak and everybody but me took a hand in cooking it for supper. Amigo couldn't make bread so I made some biscuits and cooked them in a Dutch oven. One of the things that most people don't know about making bread in camp is that you can roll the top of a flour sack down and pour whatever milk or water you are going to use with one hand and work your flour with the other hand until you have got a soft loose dough and then add the baking powder, soda, salt and lard and finish working it into your dough. The moisture will only take up the amount of flour it needs and when you finish, you can lift your bread dough out of the top of the sack and leave dry flour with little or no dough worked off into it.

I had fresh onions and these campers had some other things such as pickles. I had been killing and trapping a few blue quail which was the only fresh meat I'd had since I left Charley Green's and this venison cooked in an iron skillet with a lid on top was really good eating. We all got full of meat and bread and these three Kansas City Daniel Boones and Amigo must have drunk a big gallon of coffee. We sat around the fire and talked and visited until we were dozing off one at a time. We got up and made our beds. These rugged campers had brought a tent that they put up by the side of their pickup and had soft luxurious sleeping bags that much to Amigo's amazement, they went to bed in. He had never seen a sleeping bag and thought that was pretty rich living.

Next morning the hunters were so sore they could hardly get out of bed. They thought while they had enough gas they had better try to get back out to Cooper's Store and back to Marathon. They asked me how far it was to Marathon and I made a close guess that it was a hundred and sixty miles which really wouldn't have been too far wrong from where we were camped and the way they were going to have to try to wind around and try to follow their tracks back out of there. We had a lot of hand shakin' and they insisted that me and Amigo come to Kansas City and they would show us the sights. They bragged on Amigo for knowing exactly where the deer were and while they were all heart, Amigo bummed them out of all the rest of their coffee. As they drove away, he said, "They sure good fellows."

I told Amigo with the tourist season over we had better get back to the business of catching horses. He said that he would take Old Bay and make the round to look at his traps, so I saddled Beauty thinking if we had something caught, I could bring it in. His traps were about an hour and a half's ride from camp to the first one and the others weren't much further up — all of them set over trees in the same cedar timber. When we got to the traps, I was about ready to take Amigo in as a full partner. He had caught three of the seven two- and three-year-olds that I saw about two weeks before this. Two of them were still standing and were pretty well wrapped up in their ropes. The third one had bucked and got its rope around the tree so close to its throat that it couldn't get loose and had choked to death. I told Amigo that kind wouldn't bring much money. He said that we could use the hide to make hobbles and bridles with and he took his long straight knife out of his belt and skinned the colt while I got ropes on the other two tied to where they wouldn't choke and would do to lead them by.

I decided that leading these two would be a pretty hard job and would be awful slow so I brought one neck rope over the other colt and between dodging and fighting pulled them to where they were about four feet apart giving them enough room to travel easily and tied the rope where it wouldn't choke them and let the other rope drag. Never take off any rope you can get on a mustang when you're trying to get back to camp with them.

When Amigo had his hide wrapped and folded and tied the way he wanted it, I held the hide while he got on Old Bay that really didn't want him to carry that fresh smelling hide on him.

I untied the two colts from the tree and hazed and hollered and drove them out into the open. They got crossways of a tree or two — one on each side and I had to ride in and take one end of the rope to get him to go on the other side of the tree and when I did the other one pulled him forward in a hurry and it didn't take long to get them into the open. The two loose ends of the rope dragging scared them and they put on right smart of a run for I guess five or six miles when they decided that those ropes were going to be following anyway and they just as well settle down. We got back to camp with two two-year-old fillies that I hadn't planned on catching and the hide off of about a three-year-old that I would've been glad to have had.

Amigo took his hide and stretched it and tied it between two trees where the wind would dry it and where he could get to it to scrape fat and loose tissue off it. It was a good day's work and Amigo was prouder than I was because he had set the traps and caught three horses and seemed to be prouder of the hide off the dead one than he was with the two we got back with alive. We still had some venison left in camp that didn't go back to Kansas City and we ate a big bait of it. Amigo made his coffee and had a change of heart about me and thought it was good that I didn't drink coffee. We were both tired and give out and went to bed early.

In the night I realized it had been a mistake to have skinned that horse because the scent had rode the strong east wind until it had gathered several panthers. The carcass must have been a good ten miles from our camp, but it was down a canyon and we could hear the panthers scream and fight all the latter part of the

34

night which made me wonder if they would get brave enough to come into camp.

Next morning at breakfast I noticed Amigo making his coffee awful stout and I said, "Amigo, you gonna use up that coffee pretty fast."

He said, "Si, it take *mucho* coffee to settle my nerves after I hear them panthers all night. Maybe so they come up here."

I thought I would have a little fun out of him and said, "Amigo, when they finish up that carcass, they'll be up here next to get that fresh hide you brought back to camp."

Amigo said, "Be no fresh hide pretty soon."

I wondered what he was going to do to it, but I didn't ask. When we finished breakfast, he laid the hide on the ground and covered it about an inch deep with hot ashes and stirred them around to keep from burning through the hide. After a while he picked it up and shook the ashes off and there was nothing fresh left about that hide. He said it would take a little time to make the hide soft again, but he didn't need no panther help at what he was doing.

All the horses had been nervous ever since they could hear the panthers, and the saddle horses with one of them still wearing a bell had come in close to camp and spent the night with us instead of grazing. I caught the little strawberry roan and stuck some fresh cooked tortillas in my saddlepocket and told Amigo I wouldn't be back until about suppertime.

I rode back to the canyons and mountains where I had found the main herd of horses and rode most of the day without seeing much sign of them. I picked up their trail where they had changed range and gone south and then east into Alamo Creek which was the direction that we had caught the fillies the night before that were probably trailing the main band but I guess the running that

I had give 'em had made 'em decide to change range and I rode back into camp about dark and hadn't seen a horse.

The next morning I propositioned Amigo to ride with me. In case we found some horses he could be a lot of help. Amigo wasn't too fond of the idea and as we rode during the day, I could tell for sure that he had ridden very little and didn't fit on a horse. For whatever good he was going to be, it would have to be around camp. We found the main band of horses in the early afternoon near Mule Ear Peak. I didn't know what direction there would be a spring from there but I could tell by looking at the horses that they were watering and had found fresh range. I told Amigo to circle way around to the north while I kept their attention and when he got behind them, I would move to the south and try to drive them closer to our camp.

It seemed that they knew we were just following them and they drove pretty good but kept about a half mile distance between us and them. They stopped at a water hole at the head of Alamo Creek and it was getting too late to hope to catch any of 'em and get into camp with 'em the same day so we dropped way around and left 'em and rode into camp. I figured that since they watered there, they might spend the night and early the next morning I would try to think of something smart to catch some of these younger mares.

Amigo cooked supper and he was stiffnin' up pretty bad from the day's ride and sure wasn't a horse Mexican. We heard the cats again that night, but it didn't seem like there was as many of them or at least they didn't make as much noise. I was hoping against hope that they would go some other direction.

I left camp next morning before daylight hoping to ride on to that band of horses while they were still hungry enough to be grazing and before they went to water and started drifting. I picked

36

up their trail at the water hole and they had headed back to the upper waters of Terlingua Creek. I rode on to them pretty soon and turned them back north toward camp hoping that if and when I caught one, it would be closer to camp. When we weren't too far away from camp, the mares I had staked out must have winded this band and began to nicker and call in pretty plaintive kind of horse language which drew the attention of the mares in the lead and it looked for about an hour that I might be gonna drive 'em square dab into camp.

I got in sight of camp and still had these horses and they were still going to the call of the mares that were staked. Amigo heard us and quit whatever he was doing and dropped down a foot in the widest open place from camp thinking he might booger 'em toward the bluff and at least keep them from getting away. They drifted nearly into camp and sure enough turned the direction that

Amigo had gone. These horses had probably never seen a man afoot and Amigo scared the hell out of 'em.

I had left the two fillies in one side of the corral and the other side was open. During all this nickerin' and squallin' and commotion, some mares went over to smell them over the fence and three fat mares got themselves into the other smaller corral. I caught sight of them out of the corner of my eye at exactly the right time and hurried to put up the bars of the corral before they had time to get out. This was the biggest piece of luck that I had had, provided I got ropes on them before they demolished that little pole corral.

Of course all the rest of the horses got away and I didn't try to stop 'em. Amigo came running up waving his hands and his hat talking about how lucky we were, and I told him to get right quiet fast before he boogered them over that fence. I thought if they stayed in that corral after the other horses had gone that they might settle down enough to give me a chance to catch more than one of them before they broke out.

We waited about an hour and it was getting pretty late in the afternoon so I put Amigo on one side of the corral with a lariat rope in his hand. I realized that he might not catch anything and if he did, couldn't hold it, so I used a great long soft rope and tied it to the bottom of the best corral gate post thinking that if he did have the good luck to catch one that maybe being staked to the bottom of that gate post, it might hold her till I could get to her. We stood around the outside of the corral for a few minutes and I could see that I was going to have to rope over the fence if I stood a chance to catch more than one. That way, I was boogerin' them to keep them away from that side of the fence and Amigo was boogerin' them away from the front side. That put them against the bluff wall on the back side and the fillies on the other side.

I was riding Old Bay and I saddled Beauty before we started

this little welcomin' party for those three mustang mares. The riggin' on the old pack saddle that I put on Beauty was plenty stout but to make sure I ran the rope through the hole in the swell of the saddle and around her body and tied a smaller rope to it at the bottom of the cinch to keep it from working backward on her and brought the end of the rope back up through the swell of the saddle and double half-hitched it to the saddle horn. This gives a horse the greater advantage in that they have their entire weight to hold and pull with instead of pulling only from the saddle horn and it takes the place of having to have the stoutest riggin' in the world.

I sat on Beauty and got close to the fence, and of course, these mares were huddled up against the bluff and working their heads up and down trying to hide behind each other. In a case like this I sure wanted to rope the outside one to keep from getting too many horses over, under or across my rope. There was a bright colored sorrel filly among these three and she accidentally got herself on the outside. I dropped my loop on her and stepped off of old Beauty because I was going to be busy with the rest of them pretty quick. Beauty got the message and backed up and choked that mustang and pulled her out from the back of the corral. I spoke to her and told her that was enough and she just took a firm stand.

While Beauty was working, I got on Old Bay and by good luck had caught another mare. She rared up and busted herself against the ground and got up with the wind knocked out of her and for a few seconds wasn't much trouble and while I had those few seconds, I untied the rope from the saddle horn and tied the end of the rope to another corral post. The third mare by now had gone plum wild and started over the draw bars that we used for a gate. I squalled at Amigo that I had two and he better catch that one. In his excitement he threw a wad of rope at her that wouldn't have fitted in a pool and I don't know how, but she got her head in it. As she cleared the poles and hit the ground, I squalled at him to back up. Just in case she jerked that pole from the ground, I didn't want him to get knocked in the head. In a matter of minutes we had created a pretty big storm that was going to last for some time.

Before the two fillies tied to the horses got wrapped around each other, I went to working Beauty around the fence and flippin' the rope over the fence post and got Amigo to pull the draw bars and I drug one of the mares out in front where she choked down. I tried to get Amigo to put a hackamore on her head but his nerve failed him and she got up. It's a heap harder to choke one down the second time, but when she fell, I was on the ground and got a hackamore on her head and worked and drug her around to a good stout tree and staked her out.

By this time I was wringin' wet with sweat and about half give out so I stepped on Old Bay. The mare he was holding wasn't causing too much trouble and I waited until I got my breath to start the battle because Amigo just wasn't too much of a warrior when it came to outlaw mustangs. She made two or three big lunges and every time she did, I would take up the slack on her till I jerked her through the gate and in much the same manner got her tied to another gentle tree.

There wasn't any way to untie Amigo's mare from the bottom of that post just using one rope without standing a good chance of her getting away, so I roped and tied her to Old Bay. Then Amigo started to untie the rope from the bottom of the post but I had made a bad tie and the mare had tightened up on the rope and he was going to have to cut the rope. Even though I was pulling the mare out of the way, Amigo couldn't cut that rope for looking back to see that that mustang wasn't going to paw him to death so it took him a while to get her loose from that post.

I had to drag her a good deal further from camp than the others because we were running out of trees that were real close by and when we finally got her staked out, it was nearly dark.

I had had a few dry tortillas for dinner and Amigo nearly had a hot supper ready before I rode in and it looked like we had had a real good day.

I never knew a whole lot about the habits of Mexican panthers but Amigo said he knew all about them and that they lived on a certain kind of route over a wide area of country and would get back to where that horse carcass was in about ten days to two weeks or more and the only way you could trap or kill one was to watch the territory to see how many days again before the panthers would be back and by then you could be ready to bait or catch or poison him, but the only thing wrong with Amigo's knowledge of the cat was that he didn't know whether those cats that ate up the carcass were drifting towards the river or towards the mountains.

We hadn't much more than gotten to sleep when the ringing of that horse bell and the scream of a panther all sounded about the same time and woke us up. The horses ran right up into camp and tried to see who could get into that little corral first and Amigo seemed like he was trying to get in bed with me before I knew he was there. I don't know just what a panther would smell like getting in bed with me, but Amigo had some kind of whang that ought to have belonged to a wild animal so I encouraged him to go kick up the fire while I got my clothes on and got my rifle.

Unless there were several panthers out there, it wasn't likely that they would try to take down a grown horse like the mares that were staked out, but they sure might try the two-year-old fillies and, of course, if they got a chance to spring on that five- or six-month-old colt, it would be a sure bet that they would never miss.

41

It's always been told, and so far as I know is a sure fact, that wild animals won't come in close to a fire. When I told Amigo that, damned if I didn't think he was going to burn up the corral fence the way he went to gathering up loose pieces of wood and anything else he could find to throw on that fire.

The next time we heard the cat's scream, he was on the bluff that I had my lean-to built under which was about two hundred feet from the campfire. I was nursing a 25–35 rifle in the curve of my arm while I sat by the fire and I raised up on my knees and put the rifle on a big rock and took slow steady aim in the darkness and with the first shot tumbled that cat onto the ground about half way between where I was sleeping and Amigo was sleeping. We knew that there was more than one cat that had been feeding on that carcass because it was eaten up too quick so we sat around the fire the rest of the night wondering where the rest of them were. The staked mustangs all stood still during the night and the baby colt never left its mother and the saddle horses never left the corral. If man or beast in that camp was hungry or thirsty, they forgot about it until morning.

Next morning Amigo wanted to skin that cat and get his hide. I told him that I was sure we needed his hide for something but to get on Old Bay and drag that cat back down about where the horse carcass was before he ever let the scent of blood fill the air when he took off that hide. I didn't want bait that close to my bedroll. I left Amigo with his cat skinnin' and told him to water the staked horses.

I saddled the young bay horse and decided to make a big circle to try and find the band of mustangs knowing that they had sure gotten out of the range of those cats. It looked like my luck had about run out on figurin' any smart ways to catch horses and from now on, probably wasn't going to catch any mustangs except those that I could outrun and rope one at a time, but I had proven to myself that Charley Green and the rest of the people that let on that these might be phantom horses were mistaken to the extent of twenty-five or thirty head that was in that one stud's band.

I rode all day and came into camp after dark and hadn't seen a horse. I began to think that this stud had headed his mares further back and further up into the high country to the east and south of where I was camped. I knew that I couldn't cover a lot of country and be back at camp every night and find those horses so the next day I took a light pack which was just about half a bedroll, a skillet and enough grub to last about three days and told Amigo that he was in full charge of the camp until I got back. I had two rifles and one of them was a 30–06 with a long octagon-shaped barrel. I knew it was so big and heavy that Amigo wouldn't get far from camp with it, but it would make him feel like he could keep the boogers off. I carried my saddle rifle and left riding the young bay horse and leading the strawberry roan with the pack.

Every day when I was gone from camp, Amigo would take a horse to pack and the axe and go up in the ridge and slopes and bring in a few sotol stalks. I had told him that after the blades of the sotol were cut off that the stalks would taste awful good to a saddle horse that was kept up at night. My saddle horses didn't know anything about eating sotol and all the mustangs were staked out or tied in some manner and it was getting hard for my saddle horses to graze enough at night to hold their flesh even though I wouldn't ride the same horse but about every third day. Amigo got to chopping the sotol up pretty fine and feeding it to the little colt and it had begun to get to be a pet.

I rode high up into the mountains and found what is known as the Basin. The Basin was a big depression up in the top of the mountains and there was an opening out to the southwest now

43

known as The Window. There was a nice little dripping spring under one of the mountain peaks and the grass was good in the Basin. I camped there that night and rode up around the rim of the Basin the next morning which was high country and hard climbing on a horse. I studied the country as far as I could see and on the eastern slope, I guess a half day's ride from where I stood, I spotted the horses that at that distance looked about as big as dogs. As rough as that country is, on a bright clear morning you can almost see further than you can ride horseback in a day.

It was slow going working my way back down into the slopes and my pack horse slowed me up some. Along middle of the afternoon the wind was blowing off of me on to the horses and they caught scent of me and started drifting at a long sweeping trot towards Glen Springs. I camped at night and found them in the day and followed them three days without ever getting close enough to even disturb them. About the only thing I did on that three days' ride was keep 'em from grazing all the time.

I made it back to camp in the night of the third day's ride. I had eaten up the grub I took, worn out the horse I was using and was no better off so far as I could tell. The little strawberry roan horse had almost slid down once coming off of a high bluff and he had a shoe clicking a little when I rode into camp. I told Amigo that we would keep him up and reset his shoes the next morning.

After breakfast, Beauty came up to the corral and I gave her a handful of cold corn tortillas that she seemed to appreciate a whole lot. I intended to ride her for my next mount, but I didn't tie her up because I knew she wouldn't leave camp and if she did, would come when I called her. I had the necessary tools to shoe a horse and Amigo got them out and we got the strawberry roan out of the corral and started to pull his front shoes off and reset them. He was not lame, but when we cleaned out the frog of his

44

right front foot, a rock almost as large as my thumb fell out on the ground and showed a streak about a quarter of an inch wide and all the way through of what appeared to be pure soft yellow gold. Well, I knew right quick that that was gonna just play hell with horse huntin' for a while, if not permanently.

I started out and retracked myself the next day and if there had been any horses in the way, I wouldn't have seen them because I rode with my eyes turned to the ground. I found several places in the high slopes where the rocks were marked by the calks of a horse's shoe. I wasn't quite ready to give up on that gold mine and I spent over a week huntin' where that chip broke off that main vein which I had convinced myself might be a foot wide and a mile deep. Amigo was sort of a rock hound and he took my horseshoeing hammer and cracked all the little- and middle-sized rocks on the southeastern slope from the Basin. Well, my saddle horses got a lot of rest which I guess is all the good that came from that gold hunt. The wild mustangs had settled down and moved over to their favorite range and I decided then it was time to go back to work, but I still rode a lot with my eyes down even if I was looking for horses.

I worked against the wind and outguessed and outsmarted and outrun these horses several times and just by hard work and toughness roped seven more head in the matter of about two or three weeks. By now I had caught most of the younger fat mares and had begun to lose interest in the older mares with colts — I sure didn't need a bunch of colts.

You don't make a good outdoor man until you quit carrying a watch and lose track of the days by not having a calendar. Then time ceases to be of any particular importance. You go to bed when it's dark and get up when it's daylight and eat when you get hungry and suppose it's the right time of day. We were about out of

45

everything to eat except what game we killed and reached the point that I was going to have to go somewhere and pack in some more grub. Besides needing a few other little things like soap and mentholatum and a small amount of feed for the saddle horses, we were nearly out of flour and out of cornmeal and Amigo had suggested that we could use some of that tallow off of that horse hide that we had layed on a rock over by the bluff or he said that he thought that the fat in that cat would be good to cook with. Well, I told him to be damn careful to not cook anything that I was going to eat in either one of them as long as we had a little lard.

I began to talk to Amigo about him staying in camp and me going back to Charley Green's and on into Marathon and get a load of supplies. It seemed like Amigo had a right smart scare for being in a camp and having the responsibility of it with nobody else there. The few times that I had been gone several days at a time, I wouldn't have been surprised to have rode in and found him gone.

What mustangs I had caught had gotten fairly gentle but wouldn't do to turn loose like I did my saddle horses with a bell on because they would scatter and run so that they would never herd like saddle horses. There was never a day that I didn't ride on to one to three herds of wild Mexican burros that dollarwise were worthless, but it wasn't uncommon to see a burro with saddle or harness marks on it that some Mexican had used as long as he needed him and then turned him out. Those that had been gentle usually grazed off to themselves two or three in a bunch and a little distance away from the main herd. I decided I needed a few of them in my business and they were very plentiful so I spent about a week roping these burros. After I caught one and he choked down a little, he gave slack on the rope and got to remembering about the days he was broke and all of them that I caught would lead good after I got ahold of them. I brought them into camp and

46

hobbled them close around in the hills or sometimes put a chain on their forefeet tied with a leather strap where they wouldn't try to go very far.

I finally decided that Amigo wasn't gonna stay in camp and take care of my horses while I went to Marathon so we spent one day yoking the halter rope of each one of these mustang horses to the neck of one of those broke burros. I knew that a mustang couldn't run away with a burro and I knew that the burro would herd and drive easy and keep me from having very much trouble trailing my catch of horses out into the open country and up the road. I had seven of these burros which I tied the seven worst mustangs to and I let the other mustangs drag halter ropes long enough that they couldn't trot or run without stepping on them.

Amigo had made me four sets of hobbles out of the hide that he took off the mustang and he had cut the rest of the hide up in strips where he could carry it to use for whatever he thought about. I told him that night when he was fixin' supper to cook up a big stack of tortillas and boil him a big pot of beans that he could fill his *morral* with so he would have plenty of grub to travel on for a few days after we broke camp the next morning. That night I got all my camp and pack pretty well together except my bedroll.

We had a big breakfast by daylight next morning and Amigo helped me get what I had left to pack on the young bay horse and asked me not to tear down my lean-to. He might want to come back there and camp some more. Well, he didn't know it, but I wasn't goin' to the trouble to tear it down anyway. Up in the early part of the morning we said our goodbyes and he helped start the horses up the canyon and I left him standing on the next hill waving real big. I'm sure he went back to camp and dried his beans and packed his tortillas and his panther hide that he was probably going to tell some Mexican he caught with his own bare hands.

I rode Beauty and sat up straight and drove my stock pretty hard all day only stopping to water and shade up a little bit in the middle of the afternoon. I followed plain trails all day coming out of the Big Bend toward the public road and camped close to Grapevine Hills and found there was a little spring that would water my stock. I caught and staked the loose mares and unpacked and staked my gentle horses and left those tied to the burros to graze and turned old Beauty loose.

I rigged up early the next morning with no trouble and crossed Tornilla Creek and figured on watering again at an old mud tank that I knew about further up the road. I hadn't seen a calendar in a long time and didn't really know what month it was, but all along the road as far as I could see up the hillsides, the different kinds of cactus were in full bloom and gave a rainbow-like array of yellow, white, pink and red to the desert plant life that told me it was the late part of February or early March.

The fourth day I drove my stock into Charley Green's ranch near Persimmon Gap. We turned my world's gatherings into a little trap pasture that was about a half section and spent nearly all night telling Charley about some of the Big Bend that he hadn't had time to find in several years that he had been there. I told him I wanted to leave my horses and burros behind that fence for a few days while I went into Marathon with a couple of pack horses and got some supplies.

Charley bowed up and wanted to know what I needed to go into Marathon to get supplies for when I was on my way out with the horses I caught in the Big Bend. He said, "You don't think that you can get any more out of that small bunch that you left. Seems to me like all the supplies you need is enough grub to get you from here to town. I'll furnish you that and then you can road your horses back towards home and cook and eat along the way."

48

"Charley," I said, "this might come as some shock to you, but I aim to go into Marathon and get plenty of grub and supplies and turn back toward Maravillas Canyon and go to Stillwell and cross into Old Mexico at the Stillwell Crossing and see what kind of horses I can mustang out of Northern Mexico."

Charley was a much older man than me and the thought of me going into Old Mexico with a bunch of horses and the idea that I might get some more to bring out unnerved him way past bedtime, and I got all the sound, friendly advice that he could have possibly had stored up for everybody that he knew. Next morning I went to riggin' up to go into Marathon and he said, "When you get into town and eat a big woman-cooked dinner at the Gage Hotel and sit around in some of them rockin' chairs, don't you get tempted to just drift back into the old country and leave me with this bunch of damn worthless stock."

He may have meant this in fun, but he made it sound pretty serious. I told him that wasn't near enough horses to take back with me and as much trouble as they had caused, he could bet his last chew of tobacco that I would be back to get 'em.

I made it into town by dark that day and loafed around, visited a little and ate up some grub and let my horses rest a day. Next morning I bought up a pretty big batch of stuff — all that two horses could pack and even tied a few little things on my own saddle. I started back to Charley's, but being loaded I knew I couldn't make it all in one day so I camped at the Twin Windmills by middle of the afternoon.

I rode into Charley's next morning before noon. He was sure glad to see me because he was wondering how he could explain to his neighbors why he was winterin' a bunch of jennys and mustang horses behind a fence. I had got a few little things that he wanted and had put them handy at the top of the pack so we unpacked and unrigged my horses and spent the rest of the day around the place.

That night I told him I was getting restless and my stock was getting older and I had better drift back the next morning and get to my business of hunting horses. He said, "There's one horse in your outfit that's too good to waste down there in Mexico amessin' with mustangs. He's big and stout and gentle and I need him around here."

I knew he was talking about Old Bay and I said, "Well, Charley, you and that old bay horse are about the same speed and if you don't do anything too strainin', both of you would probably last till dinner. I'd rather trade him for money, but I know what your feelings would be about that so what do you aim to have me drive off with that you don't want anyway for the old bay?"

He said that he had a band of mares in the lower pasture and that there were some unbroke ones that he would let me pick three of them for Old Bay. I said, "Charley, I haven't seen the mares, but that ain't a very good deal cause it would take what two of 'em's worth to make up for the trouble of breaking one. But if you want to trade, we'll go down in the morning and I'll eyeball 'em and see how many of 'em it would take to get me to leave Old Bay. After all, he's fat and gentle and a pretty good friend of mine and I would kinda hate to leave him here with you where there ain't gonna be much action."

Charley's band of horses were no trouble to find the next morning and he had a set of working corrals off down in the pasture that we drove 'em in. Most of his horses were just a little better than the mustang kind because of the way he had selected 'em and maybe fed 'em a little in bad times and he had several good dun mares and yearlings and twos. I told him I guess it would take about six head to fix it to where I wouldn't grieve too much for

50

Old Bay. He said, "I'm still just gonna give you three grown mares and you can have three two-year-old dun fillies, and that's all the robbin' I aim for you to do on me."

I told him I guess I needed to do him a favor since he had been so nice to me and I would just trade with him. We cut what I wanted out and drove 'em back up to his headquarters. By the time Charley got through bragging on them mares and fillies and I quit weeping over the loss of Old Bay, half the day was gone and it was too late to pack up and start to Mexico.

Charley was doing a lot of my thinking for me or maybe he intended to find ways to keep me from going to Mexico, but he brought up the matter that whatever I drove into Mexico, I had better have a fresh Texas brand on them so that if I got into any squabble and got my horses mixed up with some other band of horses, I stood a chance of breaking even and getting the right ones back if they were fresh branded. I hadn't thought of this and about this time in my life, I had been used to winnin' most of my arguments, but it did make sense.

He had some branding irons with other figures and letters made on to the same handle, but he didn't have a plain G. We decided to heat a two-inch harness ring and use a chisel to cut it and bend it back enough to make sort of a maybeso G. This didn't take long. We used a pair of blacksmith fire tongs to take ahold of this ring and hold it on a horse till the hair burned just right to make a brand. We put the gentlest of these horses in a chute and blocked behind and in front of them with cedar poles and managed to get 'em all nearly still enough to brand 'em. Some of them flinched and jumped and we smeared a few of the brands but not bad.

We were putting this brand behind the shoulder right on the spring of the rib cage because it was an easy place to brand and would be an easy spot to see when riding through the horses. This was hard work and took all afternoon. I burned a very light "hair" brand on my saddle horses but didn't let the burn go into the hide to make a sore place. I took the ring out of the fire and after it cooled put it in the bottom of my saddle pocket in case I might need to brand some more horses.

Early next morning I got rigged out and Charley saddled Old Bay and helped me to the road with all my stock. I headed 'em south and he turned back and told me that he never expected to see me again. If the horses didn't kill me, the Mexicans would and I was a fool for not turning the other direction and going home. I thanked him for them kind words and started driftin' south.

I made it to Black Gap that night without much trouble. Of course, I already knew there was nobody at the old headquarters and there were some corrals to put my stock in. By now, my mustangs would herd and drive good and I cut the burros loose from the mares and turned them out on the Black Gap. I drove my horses down the canyon to Stillwell Crossing and made camp that night in a grassy little draw about five miles the other side of the Rio Grande River for the first time.

It was my idea that I would follow the river but stay far enough away from it that the grazing would be good and I thought I would go around the bottom end of the Big Bend and when necessary it wouldn't be too far to drift back to the river for water and cross the mountain range to the west side of northern Old Mexico. Nothing much happened for several days. The grass was pretty good and I didn't hurry my horses any and was sort of feeling my way across the vast unfenced and almost unpopulated country following the Rio Grande River.

I had seen almost no sign of horses. One day I pushed my horses into the river where the canyon walls were steep and

52

followed the water's edge through the Burro Mountains and rode close to the little town of Boquillas, Mexico. I rode around the town of Boquillas and the country had begun to be an old high rolling desert kind of country with mountain mesas sticking up here and yonder in the distance. One day during the time that I was just grazing my horses, I drifted on to a band of pretty good horses but they were all branded. They mixed up with mine and there were a few horse fights. I drifted my horses on west and cut the strange horses back and ran 'em off as I could and by middle of the afternoon had my herd back together. I guess this other bunch was on their home range but they were badly scattered.

I rode onto an open flat in between some small mountains in the late afternoon and decided it would be a good place to camp. There wasn't any water close by that I had found, but my horses had watered at a little creek during the day and I had some drinking water in a canteen so I wasn't too worried about water. I caught a few of my horses that might have roving ways during the night and staked them to small trees and yoked some of them together. I hobbled my saddle horses but left old Beauty loose. After I had my fire going pretty good, I started into my pack to get out some grub. When I moved camp I never threw out any grub that was left. I had poured my beans out on a rock at the last camp and let them dry and then wrapped them in a piece of wax paper that maybe I had already used a dozen times or so. Good wax paper or a good brown sack was scarce and I would clean 'em off and reuse them as many times as I could. I poured my beans into a pot with barely enough water out of my canteen to moisten 'em up to eat 'em and fried some good store-bought smoked bacon.

After supper I was settin' propped up against my pack and bedroll when I saw the shadow of a man slipping around among my horses. Well, I was never much afraid of a man afoot day or night that I saw on the desert. He wasn't gonna be packing any-thing that was very dangerous and he wasn't capable of carrying off much afoot. So I hollered at him to come on in to camp. He walked up very politely and took his hat off. I studied him in the flickering light of the campfire and could tell that he was a very old Mexican and had a poor mangy dog following him. He was extremely polite and used a few words of English.

I still had some beans left that were hot and I fried him a couple of strips of bacon. He ate like it was the first time in quite a spell. I cut off part of the rind of the slab of bacon and threw it to the dog. It looked like the old Mexican almost wanted to take that rind away from the dog and eat it too. Like all other stray Mexicans that I ever saw in the desert, he was carrying a *morral*, but it wasn't poochin' out much with anything. Along about bedtime I unrolled my bedroll and thought he ought to have something to wrap up in so I pitched him a ragged old horse blanket and the feed sacks that I had taken off the lean-to. He was *mucho gracias* for everything and went off about a hundred yards from camp and went to sleep.

He was up next morning early and had chucked up the fire before daylight. I thought, well, I've found another Amigo, but I hoped he knew something about a horse. When I started breaking camp, he caught on to what I was doing and asked me which horses to pack and I told him. He could put a pack on a horse that would stay there until the horse shed his hide.

In the night a mare showing a lot of age and too much breeding for a mustang, drifted into my herd of horses with about a half-grown colt that didn't show to have as much breeding as his mama which was proof enough that it was from some mustang stud. The old mare had a 7 N branded on her hip, but I couldn't drive her away from my herd and finally gave up and let her drift along.

As we started out I put the old Mexican on the strawberry roan horse bareback. He made no complaint or even asked for a saddle and I could tell in a little while that he was an old-timey horse Mexican that had probably gotten too old to stand a hard job and would make a good hand for a long time. He didn't seem to know the country too good which was a little bit of a surprise to me. We made camp early and that night he was a lot more at ease and told me that his home was way down in Mexico close to Torreón and that he was on his way to Texas to look for a ranch job and had been walking across the country twenty suns, which meant twenty days, when he walked in to my camp.

This was a big old desert country with little or no signs of game or any other kind of wildlife and I decided I had better turn west towards the mountain range in Chihuahua if I was going to find water and other horses. The next day we rode onto a little ranch run by three brothers, maybe in their thirties, and they had some horses they wanted to sell me. Well, I hadn't seen a horse that wasn't branded in about two weeks and thought to myself, if they are cheap enough I had just as soon be buying horses as trying to catch 'em.

Next day the Knoches Bros. drove their horses into an old hand-made rock corral for me to pick out what I would buy. The bunch was mixed mares and geldings. These were the first geldings that I had seen in that far Southwest country since it's not the custom to castrate stallions and it wasn't uncommon to find whole herds of studs being used for saddle horses. But I guess these brothers were a little more progressive than some of the older Mexican ranchers and all their young horses had been broken, maybe not with all the buck out of 'em, but to where they could be caught and rode and handled by cowboys. This old Mexican that had joined me was named Emundo and I asked him if he could ride these green-broke horses. He said, "Si, senor. Maybe so I would have to have a little help to get on one."

We finally got around to talking about what they wanted for their horses and the youngest one seemed to be the brains of the bunch and he did the talking. They wanted fifteen *pesos* per head for twenty geldings and ten *pesos* per head for as many mares as I would buy, and a quick count looked like they had about forty-five mares and thirty geldings but they weren't offering to sell all their geldings. I knew I would buy these horses but didn't think it would be smart to flash my money and count it out in Old Mexico in the presence of four Mexicans. Emundo, so far as I knew, seemed to be a friend, but after all, I hadn't flashed no American money in front of his eyes either.

I told them to keep these horses close where we could see 'em tomorrow and I would buy some of 'em. The exchange rate between U.S. money and Mexican money at that time was $3.68 if you were in town, and I thought I would try to trade on a basis of $4 exchange. That night in camp after Emundo went to bed, I dug down in my bedroll and saddle pockets and places where I had small amounts of money hid and scattered around and came up with enough American money to buy the twenty geldings and thirty mares. This would give me a chance to cut back fifteen and take thirty of the best ones and this would be a quick and fast way to add fifty head of horses to my bunch.

After breakfast we started back over to the ranch headquarters which was only about five miles from where we were camped By now Emundo was using a good deal more English and the old man was pretty sharp in a primitive sort of way. When I asked him if these *hombres* would take American money, he said, " Si, señor, and besides that, they'll take less for their horses if they know you are paying them in U.S. dollars."

They were riding off to bring the horses in as we rode up and they talked in Mexican and Emundo turned around and explained to me what they said. Between my little bit of Mexican and his little bit of English we were beginning to build up a new palaver that was working pretty good. I thought possibly there might be some switch in the horses that they would bring in this morning and the ones they brought in yesterday but there wasn't. There were duns and bays and browns and a few sorrels with very few white markings and no paint horses atall which made me like 'em even better.

I told them that I would buy my pick of twenty geldings and pay 'em $4 per head in U.S. dollars. Even though the young one was the spokesman, they all three spoke up at the same time anxious to take the trade when they found out it would be American money. Then I told them that I would give $3 a head for thirty mares and me pick 'em and they asked if that would be American money. When they found out it would, they were glad to make that sale too.

We were about to close the deal and start to cutting out horses when Emundo went to talking to them about a *factura*. I turned to Emundo and asked, "Which one of these horses do you think is named *factura*?"

He told the brothers what I said and everybody had a big laugh except me, but these brothers were on the up and up and so was Emundo. After a good deal of hand waving and palaver in their English and my Mexican, I gathered that a *factura* was the same as a bill of sale but had to be issued by the local *politico* in some nearby small town. Emundo had turned out to be a legal advisor as well as a cowboy and good cook and I was surprised that he knew about a *factura* because I sure didn't and it would just make the difference of whether I owned the horses or not.

58

The brothers had a little pow wow among themselves and before they rode to Carrizal where there was a government *politico* that could issue a *factura*, they wanted to see what horses I was going to take and wanted to know if I had the *dinero* to pay for 'em. Emundo translated all this for me. However, I had already caught on to what they were talking about so I told Emundo that we would cut out the horses and I would give them a dollar a head in money and pay them the rest when they came back from town with the *factura*. This was all good so as I pointed out the geldings, they roped them and put them in another small corral. As we started picking the mares, I told Emundo to pick the first fifteen and I would pick the last fifteen. This made him feel real big and he did a good job of picking out the average or better of the bunch.

By the time I had picked my fifteen we had the little corral too full of horses. I unbuttoned my left shirt pocket and gave the youngest brother five $10 bills. There was a lot of ohin' and ahin' and hurrahin' and carryin' on in fun and the youngest brother that I had paid the money caught a fresh horse and started to Carrizal to get a *factura* and said he would be back the next day after dinner time.

We talked about keeping these horses up all that time in this small corral. There weren't near as many horses left that they were keeping as those I had bought, so the other two brothers and Emundo agreed that we would keep up the horses I didn't buy and turn the ones I did buy back out on the range and gather them again the next day. The oldest one of the brothers that had had very little to say said to be sure everybody was treated fair that he thought we should take a pocket knife and bob about four inches of hair off of the end of the tails of the ones I was buying. This sounded awful good to be coming from a Mexican doing business with a *gringo* where they had practically all the odds if they would have cared to use them. It didn't take but a little while to bob these horses' tails as they were gentle to catch and we turned them out. Me and Emundo had dinner with them and then rode back to our own camp.

We weren't too far from a small stream called Rio Conchos which they told us was about fifty miles from Ojinaga across the river from Presidio, Texas. Well, you could have fooled me because I really didn't know where I was. Emundo and me drove all of the horses to the river and watered them close to where we had crossed two days before, and Emundo grazed and held the herd in the draw. I rode back to camp and late in the afternoon Emundo brought them into hobble and stake and put up for the night. By now, Emundo was doing nearly all the cooking and since he had got full, he was giving the bacon rind to the mangy dog without showing that he wished the dog didn't eat so much.

Next morning we had finished breakfast and were brushing our saddle horses for the day before we saddled up when one of the brothers rode into camp to tell us that the other brother had gotten back early and they were ready for the rest of the money. I told them that was good, only I was ready for the horses first. We rode back with him to their headquarters about the time that they were to bring the horses into the corral. I had begun to think about that branding business, so after they had the horses in the corral, I got out of my right shirt pocket the $80 I owed them and showed that I had a $5 bill left in my pocket. Before we left camp that morning I took my branding iron out of my saddle pocket and explained to Emundo that we ought to brand these horses. I told the brothers about my brand and Emundo explained it to them. I said I would give them this last $5 to brand the horses. Well, that was about eighteen *pesos* and looked like big pay so they started building a fire and roped each one of these horses by

60

the forefeet and tied 'em down and then branded them on the rib cage on the left hand side. We stopped for a mess of beans and tortillas and since they were doing this the slowest hardest way, we had 'em all branded by middle of the afternoon and drove 'em to our camp.

I knew they wouldn't get far, but if they did go back home, we would have to gather them again so we yoked several of them to our horses and staked out about half of them thinking that that would hold the rest around the herd till morning. I knew I would have to move herd fast to get these horses off their home range to where they would stay with us and I talked about it that night to Emundo. Since we were headed west and had begun to be able to see a mountain range probably a week's ride in the distance, we got up early and pushed the whole herd to get them tired so that they would drive easy and stay together. I guess we made about twenty-five miles that day and camped just before dark.

We hadn't crossed water all day and found a small watering place in the desert that would water all the horses, but they left it pretty nasty for us, and our canteen water was getting kinda low. Emundo thought that the water and the fact that the horses were all tired would hold them together pretty good, but I insisted that we stake a few of the new bought horses and hobble our saddle horses and that he had better stake a night horse. The mare that I caught back in the Big Bend that had the little colt was bad to take her colt and get out of the herd so I told him to catch her and stake her too. The two-year-olds that I had gotten from Charley Green and the two-year-olds that we had trapped had sort of formed their own little bunch and stayed together but always a little ways away from the main part of the herd and I thought about breaking them up but I didn't do it. This had been a hard day's work and we were about as tired as the horses were so after eating a batch of camp grub, both of us went to sleep pretty quick.

We weren't near to the mountains yet, but were in a little rougher country than the desert that we had crossed during the day and sometime in the late part of the night two panthers came in close to camp and screamed real loud which was all that was needed to get me out of my bedroll fast and Emundo was wanting a rifle. I gave him the big rifle and I took the saddle rifle. Our horses were already excited and had begun to scatter when the cats bounced out of the darkness onto the colt and the cats had the colt killed in less time than it takes me to tell it.

The night wasn't pitch dark and I could see the form of horses running different directions and the old hobbled mare was trying to fight the cats with her hind feet. I couldn't get a chance to shoot for a good bit because of horses being in the way and when I did get to open fire, the cats were scared away by the commotion we were making, but the colt was already dead. I called Beauty and in the excitement she knew that things were bad and was standing almost over my bedroll. I saddled her fast and got on her and took the light rifle and intended to track the cats but that was a lost cause in the dark. Emundo had caught the strawberry roan and we spent the rest of the night and the early morning hours trying to regather my band of not-so-tired horses as we had thought. When we finally made a drive from each direction and brought in what we had to camp, we accounted for most all of them except the two-year-olds that didn't stay with the main herd and probably had turned back in the direction we brought 'em.

When we started to change horses I told Emundo that we needed to start using some of the new horses that we bought and give the other horses some rest. He said that was good and picked up a rope and walked into the herd and caught a big brown gelding that was supposed to be broke. He snorted and ran backward and

62

choked a little but Emundo didn't have too much trouble leading him out of the herd. Emundo said that he thought the horse was broke to ride, but that the Knoches Bros. must not have known about the wild hairs and he would have to pull them out. I had heard about all kinds of superstitions and sayings, but I didn't know about wild hairs. He got a hackamore on this fresh horse and told me that as soon as he got the wild hairs pulled out he would be all right. I still don't know about this pullin' wild hairs but thought I would wait and find out.

There are a few long guard hairs around under a horse's eyes and on his face and there are also some guard hairs around under a horse's mouth and under his lip. Emundo didn't bother any of the guard hairs around the nose and lip but he took his finger nails and was pullin' the long guard hairs out of the face that grows an inch or so below the eyes. Of course when he got ahold of one of these deep-rooted larger hairs and jerked it real quick, the horse would run backward and have another fit. Emundo kept on until he had about half of these long guard hairs pulled out of the horse's face under both eyes. Then he led him up to where I had saddled my horse and held by the cheek of the hackamore and went to saddling his horse. He told me there were lots of people that didn't know about pullin' the wild hairs out of a horse's face and that the horse was broke now. I wanted to laugh or make some kind of smart remark but I didn't. I said, "I'm sure glad that you showed me. From now on when I'm going to ride a bad horse, I'll pull the wild hairs out of his face."

He told me the horse would be *poco* gentle and it seemed that it did Emundo more good than it did the horse because he just cheeked him and stepped on him knowing that there was nothing bad left in the horse. I thought to myself, the horse could grow some more guard hairs and if it gives a cowboy that much more courage maybe I might learn to spread the word when I was getting somebody to ride broncs.

We fixed a fast breakfast, changed horses and Emundo held herd and tried to get the horses settled down to graze and suck at that muddy water hole while I turned back east to overtake the two-year-olds. They were about a two hour's ride from camp and had found a glade to graze in even though they were just getting a bit of grass between looking over their shoulders for anything bad. When I came into sight of them they broke into a run and it took about three or four miles to pass 'em and turn 'em back. I pushed them back into the main herd in the early afternoon.

We had to move camp fast to get away from the carcass of that colt and find a new spot that my horses might settle in for the night because they were sure going to be on the booger all night if we stayed there. We made it to some low rolling hills and made dry camp. However, our horses had had water and after the mud hole had settled, we had gotten some water that would do to drink so I didn't think one dry camp would hurt us too much. During all the night's and day's excitement the horses hadn't grazed very good and nothing was full and I hoped that they would graze instead of drift but it was too much of a chance to take. Emundo rode herd till about middle of the night and he had to push these horses several times to keep them from turning back to the east and north. I had rode Beauty pretty hard but I knew this was the kind of night all hell might break loose so I saddled her again and kept the horses together pretty well until after daylight. By this time, even with a rider and holding and turning them back all night, they had easily worked themselves a mile and a half away from where we had stopped for camp.

A little after daylight Emundo rode in and said he had left hot

64

breakfast and he would watch the horses while I went to eat. I don't know what boogered 'em but the whole herd came up behind me runnin' top speed before I had time to get to camp. We managed to turn them in a mill until they ran themselves down and pushed them back in the foothills west of where we were camped and I went to get breakfast. After I finished breakfast and went back to the herd, I sent Emundo back to break camp and pack two of the horses that we had left staked and he could catch up with me since I thought it best to let these horses go to driftin' if they would go to the west and get further away from their home range and two bad nights.

As I started pushing them, I discovered that we were in more trouble. While we were holding herd that night two of the Charley Green mares had brought baby colts. Nobody knows how far a wobbly-legged baby colt can travel after it's gotten up and got full of mama's milk. It is true that these mares drop back to the tail of the herd but these little wobbly-legged colts kept up close to their mama's flanks all day and occasionally we stopped and let the little things nurse and rest but it was plain to see that nature had provided a baby colt with enough stamina for a mare to move it a long ways the first day or night if it had been born in unfriendly territory infested by animals of prey. Along in the afternoon the whole band settled down and were grazing and drifting very slowly and the mares with the colts stopped long enough for the babies to lie down and get a little bit of that baby rest and stretch out on the ground under the warm sun.

About a half a mile off to one side to where we were passing, there were four rather old looking jennys with colts of various ages from little to about half-grown. I loped over and pushed them into my herd. Few people know that a panther prefers any kind of jenny meat to that of horse meat and the greatest delicacy that you can tempt a panther with is a burro colt. I was in hopes that we had outrode the panthers, but in case we hadn't, I was going to try to bait them with a burro instead of those two baby colts that had been born on the drive.

I told Emundo to ride around the herd and stop 'em at a little clump of trees that I could see in the distance which on the desert would be a good sign that there would be a water hole there. Sure enough, under the clump of big trees was a nice clean spring not very big but with awful good water. Emundo came back in a lope to get the canteen and camp water can and wash it out and get it full of fresh water before the horses got there. Since we had drove pretty hard all day, everything was thirsty and the lead horses smelled water and almost beat Emundo back to the spring but he managed to get a big drink and get the canteen and can full before the herd took over the spring. The jennys and their colts were the last things to water and the way they picked out a tree and went over under it to shade together, made me think it might be their home range and the place where they were used to watering.

Emundo was making camp back a little piece from the spring under two small liveoak trees. I drove these jennys hardly a mile away from the herd and shot a jenny colt to bait the cats with to keep them off of my horse colts. When I rode back, Emundo wanted to know what the rifle noises was about and I told him thinking it was good common sense and he would understand. He went into a wild mad fit telling me that the jennys were just as valuable to man as the horses were, and he went on to tell about what all the burro had done to help man in the desert. The more he talked the madder he got, and he told me that any man that would shoot a burro colt was a brother to the wolf and he was leaving.

I tried to explain it to him and that didn't do any good, so I tried joking him out of it and get him to stay. It was no joke.

66

I told him to get plenty of frijoles and tortillas if he was leaving camp so he would have something to eat on. When he got ready to leave the little mangy hairless dog that had had more fat bacon rind than he had had in all of his life decided to stay with me, much to Emundo's disgust. He walked out of camp about dark and I felt like he might be back for breakfast, but I never saw him again. This left me with lots of trouble and lots of horses.

Not too late in the night I heard a cat scream and picked up my saddle rifle. I didn't bother to get a horse and sneaked out into the night to where I had shot the burro colt. Luckily the cats had only screamed once when they found the colt and were busy eating it when I got there. I sneaked up by the side of a small gnarled little tree and rested my rifle on a limb, took dead aim and shot them both before they could get away. However, I didn't kill the second one I shot and I cautiously slipped up on him and shot him a few more times. I figured when I got back to camp I would be afoot and all my horses scattered and gone but since the cats never got into the horses and the wind was against them, the horses didn't smell them so they had caused very little commotion and stayed together pretty good till morning.

I was camping at a good spring of water and felt like there would be some local ranchers calling on me in a few days to move my herd away from that spring, but the more I rode in the next few days the more I realized that this range wasn't stocked with anybody else's livestock. I thought I would stay and graze these horses and get 'em more used to being together and get over the scare they had while I tried to figure out which direction to go and too, I wanted to ride out the surrounding country for either mustangs or owned horses that I might buy cheap.

After I had been camped about a week, I had two stray riders, not riding together but on the same day, come into camp and ask for something to eat. They were friendly and didn't savvy much English and I didn't let on like I savvied much Mexican. One of them needed a horseshoe and I had one about the right size and helped him put it on his horse.

While we were shoeing his horse, the Mexican noticed a young mare that had come back to water instead of grazing with the rest of the bunch. Her front leg was swelled pretty bad just above the knee and she was barely putting that foot on the ground. He pointed to it and began explaining by signs, motions and broken Mexican and English that the Spanish dagger plant that was growing nearby was good for the snakebite. After he said this, I remembered seeing a handful of Spanish dagger plants laying in the rock corral fence at the Knoches Bros. and wondered then what they were for. They were tied together with a rawhide string and all the points were sticking one way.

This drifting Mexican cowboy took his knife and went to cut about twenty Spanish dagger plants about a foot long that had points on the end of them. While he was doing this, I eased around and dropped a rope on the mare. She wasn't too wild and didn't offer to fight too much. I had gotten her up and tied her to a tree when the Mexican came back to camp with this bundle of daggers. He pulled some hairs out of the mare's tail and made a string and tied it real tight around the handful of daggers making a small bundle with them that drew the points real close together and they were all sticking out about the same distance. He explained to me what he was going to do in broken Mexican and English and I used more of the same kind of conversation and told him that I'd take a rope and tie the mare's hind foot to her shoulder where she couldn't paw or get away and then he could treat the swelling in her leg.

This didn't take long between the two of us. Then he took his pocket knife and hurriedly trimmed the worst of the long hair off

68

the swollen leg. He wrapped his bandana around the dagger plants where he could hold them without the edges cutting into his hand and he jobbed the dagger points into the leg about three-quarters of an inch deep and jerked them out just as quick as he had jobbed them into the skin. He did this all over the mare's foreleg and no telling how many hundreds of little bitty fine holes it made. Since the leg was swollen, hardly any blood came through these fine holes but a greenish-like serum seeped through and wet her leg and began to drip off. He raised up and threw the daggers away and told me that the pain of the snakebite would come out of the dagger holes and that the leg would go down in a few days. He tried to tell me that if the hair came off, it wouldn't make any difference because it would grow back.

It seemed that me and him had performed some neighborly deeds for each other and we shook hands and he rode off. The next morning the swelling was almost gone out of the mare's leg and in four or five days the hair peeled off and fresh hair began to grow back and her leg was as good as it was before she met up with the rattlesnake. Experiences like this made me wonder if there was anything actually worthless growing in the desert.

These two Mexicans was all the company I had until one morning about the time I started to drift my horses south where the grass was pretty good, a company of six Mexican rangers rode up to my band of horses and circled them and held them up. They were all dressed in the army uniform and riding better than average Mexican horses. The *Capitan* rode around and introduced himself to me. Of course, he could readily see that I was a *gringo* and that I was in possession of lots of Mexican horses. He asked me a few polite questions in fairly good English. Then he finally came to the point of wanting to know if I had a *permitir* to be mustanging horses in Mexico.

69

Well, I doubt if anybody had ever heard of a *permitir* to mustang horses but I guess that was his first thought to exercise a little authority. I reached in my shirt pocket and brought out the *factura* that I had on the fifty head. He looked at this and said that it was all right but that I had more than fifty head. He had also noticed that I had the same brand on all of them but what was the explanation for the rest of the horses? I started to explain that I had brought some saddle horses with me from Texas, and he knew which ones those were at a glance and said there were still some Mexican mustang horses that I needed a *permitir* for. Suddenly I caught on to what he was talking about and went to digging into one of my saddle pockets. I brought out a greasy brown sack full of parched corn and offered him some and he said, no, he wanted to see the *permitir*. So I kept diggin' telling him I had a *permitir*.

From the bottom of my saddle bag I brought out a small little bundle about the size of my little finger which was wax paper with a rubber band around it. I undid it and unfolded a U.S. $20 bill which was a gold certificate and one side was gold-colored. I handed him this $20 gold certificate and he turned it over a time or two and felt of it and I asked, "*Capitan*, is it made out right and in proper order for you to accept?"

"Si, señor," and he folded it and stuck it in his vest pocket and waved his men to let the horses go. I told him I had one mare branded different from the rest and from her appearance was a horse of considerable breeding and she had a unbranded colt with her. I told him about her drifting into my horses and I was unable to drive her off for more than a little while at a time and she would come back. I showed him the mare and brand. He said it was all right for me to have her — that many years before this there had been a drouth north of the Rio Grande and some Texas ranchers had pushed a bunch of horses across the river and abandoned them

70

and there were still a few scattered around on the range and this mare was one of them. I told him that the brand was a 7 N, but he wasn't particularly interested and said maybe so. Many years later I told Gid Reding about this experience and he said he was working for the ranchers that pushed that range band of horses across the river during the drouth of the 20s and said that the brand was not a 7 N but a 7 half H brand, and these horses did have a lot of thoroughbred blood in their background.

I asked the *Capitan* for a note from him giving me the right to be in Mexico buying horses since he had my *permitir*. He reached in his shirt pocket and brought out a small notebook. This *Capitan* was pretty sharp because he still remembered my name on the *factura* and he wrote out "Ben K. Green" and in big capital letters "O K" and signed his name to it as *Capitan*. I folded it and put it in my pocket and we both smiled as we shook hands and he and his men rode off.

I don't know how many days I camped at that spring but I guess it was more than two weeks and my horses had eaten the grass out pretty short and I decided it was time to move. It was a warm almost summer day and I brought my horses into water early in the afternoon so I could spend the rest of the day getting my camp together where it would be ready to pack the next morning. By now I had used some of the horses that I had bought and they were fairly good riding horses and the ones that I had packed were good pack horses. They were a little smaller than the rest of my horses so I broke my camp into smaller packs and used four horses instead of two so they wouldn't be carrying too much for their size and I needed to pack a couple of fresh ones before I tried to ride them the next day. Any time I decided I would take one of these horses for a riding horse, I would use him a day or two to pack on to take the buck out of him to where he wouldn't be too fresh when I started to ride him.

We started drifting towards the west and maybe were turning a little north at the same time. It was a big old flat country with greasewood and black brush and a few mesquite trees and the further I got away from the spring the fewer mesquites there were. By late afternoon I hadn't found any good place to camp but did ride into a little draw that had a good stand of burro grass and some small brush that was fair browse for the horses. I let them

72

stop in the draw and I picked out a little knoll that was kinda clean of brush to make my camp on. Since I was by myself I hobbled and staked a good many of the horses to kind of hedge against trouble and be sure that I would have plenty of using horses the next day that I could get ahold of easy.

My horses weren't too thirsty and didn't drift too much in the night and those that did, drifted the direction that we were going and I picked them up as I pushed the rest of the horses west. I had some fried corn and had some dry cooked beans and some tortillas left from breakfast so I didn't hold these horses up anywhere to try to build a fire and fix dinner at noon. The quality of the country wasn't improving much and I could still see mountains but they were far in the distance and that night I made another sort of bad kind of camp. I drank up my canteen water at supper and my horses had begun to show that they were drawn and needed water. This was two days that I hadn't found a water hole.

I didn't drive over seven or eight hours the next day and my horses were beginning to look real hard and nicker and complain and not graze much and I was getting pretty dry myself. This was the third night that we made dry camp and I was sure thirsty. I couldn't eat very much of that old hard camp grub because I couldn't get it wet enough to swallow. I got off to sleep and it was a bright cold desert night and just about daylight I woke up and was lying in my bedroll looking out across some pretty sorry old gravelly ground and here came a jackrabbit hopping along licking dew from the slick leaves of grass and cactus and getting all the water he needed. I thought to myself that I ought to have had as much sense as a jackrabbit, so I got up and tried licking some vegetation and some rocks and got enough moisture to wet my mouth and lips but not enough to swallow.

My horses were scattered on out west of me grazing and chewing on things so I broke camp and rigged up and actually just started following them without putting any push on them to travel very fast. The sun was out and I don't guess it was real hot but when you're dry for three days any kind of sun is hot. Late that afternoon I saw some very small mesquite trees around in the black brush and the burro grass draws. A mesquite bean will not germinate on the dry open desert until it's passed through the bowels of an animal and gotten real good soft and swelled up and then deposited on the ground in a pile of moist manure. Range horses eat mesquite beans more than any other animal and horses seldom range farther than one day away from water and when you are in the desert and find some small mesquite sprouts you can nearly bet that it's not more than a day's ride to water.

That night when I made camp I took my yellow slicker and spread it out on a flat spot on the ground and put rocks on the edge of it to hold it down flat. The cold desert nights condensed what moisture there was in the atmosphere and next morning I used my finger and led the dew that had fallen on my slicker around in little pools. I made wrinkles in the slicker to catch it and after about thirty minutes of playing around on top of that slicker with one finger I had led enough water into wrinkles to get one big tin cupful that I drank very slowly while I sat on a rock. I rolled the slicker inwardly and held it on an angle and dripped out about another half cupful that I poured in my canteen to have sometime during the rest of the day. The slicker was still damp and I held it up to Beauty's nose and she finished lickin' it dry.

When I went to trying to see my horses, I realized that most of them had drifted on west so I started pushing the strays and those that were tagging along behind and as we rode on the mesquite got bigger. A little after the middle of the day judging from the sun, the horses found a nice clear spring coming out from under a bluff in the foothills of the mountains. Me and them spent the rest of the day taking time about watering at the spring, and of course, they weren't any trouble to get to shade up around the large mesquite trees and graze for the night.

This was a little rougher and better grazing country. Since I had pushed these horses far enough so that none of them were near their home range, I decided I would camp there a few days and let everything fill up and rest from the several days I had put on them since the night of the cats. Having met the Mexican *Capitan* and knowing whose territory I was in, I felt a small amount of range security and thought it would be all right to use up a few days of my welcome. This gave my best saddle and pack horses a chance to rest and me a little time to cook some better kind of grub. I trapped a mess of blue quail one afternoon late and had all the fresh quail for supper and breakfast that I could eat which was a welcome change from that slab of salt pork that I had been dining on. As I handled and rode the geldings I got from the Knoches Bros., they all turned out to be gentle and good horses giving me a lot of riding horses where I could rest my own standbys especially when we were in camp and grazing in one place for a few days.

Since I was in rougher country I didn't have as much fear of not finding water and I wasn't finding any horses so I broke camp in a few days. In the rough terrain of the desert of Mexico there are little stores called commissaries and maybe two or three houses. I wondered how come they were there and still more, how they could manage to stay, but the merchants were generally old men with lots of patience and time and not exactly burned up with ambition. Their stock of merchandise might be meager, but still they would have the bare necessities that the people in that region would need. In my riding around over the roughs I had found such a little store and not far from it an open spring and made camp for a few days, and I restocked on the kinds of grub that I was running low on. There were just a few 'dobe houses in the foothills close to this commissary and the men began to visit with me a little bit and told me that further west in the mountains in the Yaqui country there were a good many wild horses. The Yaqui don't use horses — they were footback Indians but at the same time had kept most everybody from trapping too very many of these horses at a time. This sounded like good information and my horses had grazed several days and filled up and pretty well tromped up and muddied the spring where I really needed to move camp again. Besides that, one of the native men that had come to my camp had took a liking to the old skinny 7 half H that had the big colt old enough to wean. Of course he didn't offer any money whether he had it or not, but wanted to trade for the mare. I asked him what he had to trade in the way of horse stock and he didn't seem to have any horses. Early next morning he brought a good big Mexican handwoven blanket that was fresh washed to camp and wanted to trade it for the mare. Well, the mare was a good deal less than nothing and I was heading towards the mountains where it might get cold so I told him we would catch the mare, and I would catch and halter the colt and keep it and we had a trade. I didn't feel like I had been out anything when I swapped the old mare and after all it was a big pretty Mexican blanket. By middle of the day half the Mexican men in the settlement had brought some part of their life's household gatherings to my camp to trade for horses and since I didn't have any more mares that I thought as little of or that cost as little as the old 7 half H mare, it seemed time to move camp.

I had been climbing into higher elevation for several days and by now I was in the foothills of a mountainous region about two hundred miles south of the New Mexico-Arizona border and west of Casa Grande, Mexico. At the time I was guessing where I was but this was a close guess. I found a nice running stream coming from higher in the mountains that stayed clear and clean. The grass was good and there were a few large red pine trees that would probably take two men holding hands to reach around one of them.

After me and my horses had had plenty of water to drink, I decided I'd get sanitary and put out about a four- or five-month wash. I didn't have that many clothes with me. What I had just had that much wear and dirt on them. You never wash in a desert spring where the water isn't running because of ruining the water to drink, and this was the first running water I had found. I scared up a bar of soap out of my pack and didn't expect to have any company or passersby, so I stripped down to my boots and washed all my clothes in the spring and rubbed them on a big rock to un-pack some of the dirt and grease. I imagine I was a right pretty sight out there in the nude with just my boots and hat on putting out my wash. I even went to the trouble to wash out my best saddle blankets. I didn't use soap on them but I got lots of sweat and dirt and hair off of them. I left them till last. After all, I wanted to wash my "dainties" first and certainly before I surprised that hairless, but now fat, Mexican dog that had preferred to stay with me instead of Emundo, with a bath. Before he knew what was happening I grabbed him real quick and smeared soap all over him and throwed him in the creek. This sure did seem to be a shock to him. He came out on the bank and shook himself real good and went off to stay with the horses instead of coming to camp with me.

It was a high dry climate and my clothes dried quick. I spread them around on some rocks to sun and decided I'd pull my boots off and take a bath in that spring myself. It sure was cold in that spring water, but when I got out it was even colder when that wind hit me without that four-month cake of dirt I'd been wearin'. But by night I was a nice clean boy dressed in fresh clothes, and I had a big supper and went to bed.

It had begun to be summertime and this high cooler country was a lot better in the daytime and awful cold at night — a combination that's hard to beat when you're living out doors. Game was plentiful and grazing was good and I lost track of time riding among my horses just keeping them pushed into a range close to camp and letting them spread out and graze.

I knew I must be close to the Yaqui but didn't know how close and nobody came along for a good many days that I could ask. I was turning Mexican myself pretty fast because I began to like my *siesta* which means eat all you can in the middle of the day and sleep long as you can. One day I hadn't unrolled my bedroll and was just leaning up against it asleep when three Mexicans rode up horseback. One of them was wearing a soldier's cap but the rest of his clothes and the other's too were just common white Mexican shirts and pants. Hadn't any of them got down on the ground and I had woke up but hadn't tried to get on my feet and was just settin' there when the one with the military cap asked me about my *permitir*. I looked at him pretty good and asked him where his authority was. He patted his pistol and said, *" Esta pistola."*

I had dropped my hand down under my saddle laying next to my bedroll and told him that in a case like that my authority was just as good as his was. He and his two Mexican henchmen had a pretty loud palaver about what to do with me and finally turned and rode off. I decided it would be smart to move higher up into the mountains to fresh grass and cooler weather and since I had plenty of broke horses I packed several horses but not very heavy so they could travel light in the high country.

Sometime in the second day I rode onto another one of these commissaries. The land was open around there and I let my horses spread out and graze some of them layed down to rest and shaded up. It was a real peaceful country and the animal life, as well as the old man running the commissary, seemed very much at ease. He was a short, fat, old Mexican with a little goatee, a bright eye and big smile and seemed to like his lot in life. I got acquainted with him and bought a few little things. While I visited with him, I told him about the Mexican bandits. He fell over on the little short counter and laughed and laughed, wiped tears out of his eyes and sat back down on the box behind the counter and finally got his breath and told me that the *banditos* came by his store and wanted to buy some *pistola* bullets on credit. He knew that they weren't armed — they couldn't rob him and he refused to sell them any on credit and that's why it was so funny to him that they never did draw but rode off. Well, to add to the enjoyment of the occasion I told him when I had stuck my hand under my saddle, I didn't have a pistol at all, and we both had a big laugh.

We visited a long time and I decided I'd better make camp for the night. I walked out to where I had my horse tied and if this little old Mexican had been tall enough he would have reached around my shoulders, but he was reaching far as he could and patted me on the back and told me to camp along the creek that ran behind the store as long as I wanted to stay. My horses were staying together good and were on good water so for the next few days me and the old storekeeper visited a lot and got real good acquainted. This was the first time I had been close to a calendar since I left Charley Green's and I found out that it was early July.

I began to ask about the Yaqui and the wild horses. He seemed to know all about both and told me that there would probably be a Yaqui runner come into the commissary sometime in the next few days and he would find out how they would feel about me running and trapping some wild horses. It was generally known that the Yaqui were hostile against invaders that came to hunt and trap game and they took a dim view of any sort of white man being in their territory thinking that he might be intending to take advantage of them in some manner.

We had become good friends and I was callin' him General and he called me, Benito, by this stage of the visit. I had met his wife in the store one day. She was a lighter complexioned Mexican than the General, very intelligent looking and spoke very proper English, but as our conversation continued, I realized she didn't know very much Texas English. Then the General told me she had been a schoolteacher and taught English in Chihuahua City when she was a young woman and that was when I realized why her phraseology and words were so pure and perfect. This caused me to have to watch myself and use good English when I was talking to her. Their son and his family lived in Hermosillo and were coming for a visit and they invited me to come for dinner with them at noon on Sunday. I could see the General was very anxious for me to meet his son and grandchildren and I knew I would enjoy some real good cooking so I asked what time they would like for me to be there. The old general beamed and said, "Come early and stay late." But I didn't quite do that.

About an hour and a half before time to eat I put on what good clothes I had and walked up in the yard. The whole family came out on the porch to greet me and they were a nice looking bunch of young people. His son may have been thirty and his wife was about the same age. They had three pretty good size kids and the youngest one was two or three years old. We menfolk and kids stayed out on the porch where it was cool and visited while the women fixed dinner. Several times I heard somebody say "Chicago!" during the morning and I finally figured out that it was somebody's name. I asked the General who was Chicago and he laughed real loud and pointed at the little one. He was a round-faced bright looking kid and just beamed everytime his name was called. I asked how come they named him Chicago. They said he was born in the United States when they made their trip to the Chicago World's Fair and they were just real proud to explain that he was a U.S. citizen and a Mexican citizen too. Well, I didn't know that much about citizenship, but I had a big laugh over it and they thought it was funny that I thought it was funny.

After a big dinner of real good Mexican grub everybody scattered to take their *siesta*. I went back to my camp and the General said they would see me after awhile. In the cool of the afternoon here came the General and his son and all the little boys to ride a horse. Of course I put them on old Beauty without a saddle and just stacked them from her ears to her tail. They thought that was big fun, but after awhile the oldest boy decided he would quit riding and catch a fish out of the spring. He put a little piece of meat on a bent pin and the spring was so clear and pretty that he could see fish and dangle that meat in front of them. The land was so fresh and unspoiled and the fish so well fed that they didn't pay any attention to his bait and that upset him considerably. He caught a large bug and put on his hook and we stood and looked through the water and watched a big fish eat the bug off the hook without ever swallowing the hook. This was the nicest Sunday I had had since I had that raisin pie at the Gage Hotel in Marathon, Texas, about five months ago.

I had been camped there about three weeks and me and the General were settin' on the front porch with our feet hanging off. His feet wouldn't touch the ground he was so short and I said, "General, I thought you were gonna have a Yaqui runner in here by now."

He laughed and said, "Benito, there was a Yaqui man here several days ago but I did not tell you because I think maybeso you stay no longer and we enjoy your company."

I asked him what did the Yaqui think about me drifting my horses over into their part of the mountains and trapping some of the wild horses. He said that he told the Yaqui I was a good fellow and he knew I had *dinero* because I had put it in his safe. You see, when I got there and found out he was a pretty good Mexican, to ward off any temptations that some of the natives might have to rob me, I put part of my money in the General's safe in the commissary. He was real proud of me for that.

The Yaqui runner had told the general if he did not hear from them in three days that he could tell me it would be all right to move into their mountain range. I asked the General how many days had it been? He said, "Oh, Benito, it has been a week. I just didn't want to cause you no hurry."

It took me about a day to get my camp together the way I wanted to pack it. I packed each horse light so that they could travel in the high country and early one morning I rode up to the commissary to get my money and tell the General goodby. When I told him what I wanted he said, "If I no let you have your money, you no leave," but laughed when he said it and went and opened the safe and handed me my money in the same bundle that I had handed it to him in. I dropped it in my coat pocket without bothering to undo and count it, and the old General shook hands with me and said, "You no even count your money. You are one good *gringo* and maybeso you come back and camp with us some more."

I had my horses pretty well rounded up and started driftin'

them out from behind the store and the old General and his wife stood on the porch and waved and hollered *hasta la vista* until I was out of hearing distance.

I got into some real high country with very few trails and began to wonder whether I was going across the mountains or up the range on the east side. I finally ran into a fairly well-blazed trail that I think probably wagons had used a little and it was easy for my horses to follow this trail through a pass. I came out on the high country on the west side of the mountain range and in two or three more camps, I was in a high prairie country with lots of fine timber, good grass and cold running streams. I had drove and loose herded my horses until they all knew to stay pretty well together and even though they would scatter out to graze, they would be in small bunches and in sight of each other and I made a habit of pushing them back toward camp in the late afternoon to get them to graze and bed close to the creek during the night. I hadn't planned it but I had made this drive to where the weather had been ideal. It was August and I was high up in the mountains in cool country and almost in sight of the deserts where the temperature might have been 110 degrees.

My little hairless dog had begun to look better and his skin was getting oily since I had soaped him and throwed him in the creek. I thought he was the most useless dog I had ever seen because he wouldn't bark at a horse, varmit or stranger, but one thing about him, he didn't make a nuisance of himself rubbing up against me wanting to be petted. He stayed well back from the fire at camp and out of the way of the horses when I was saddling or unsaddling.

It was late afternoon and I had made a good comfortable camp and was leanin' back on a big rock to rest when over to one side of camp in a pile of rocks I heard the dog growling in a deep tone like he had something cornered. Since I'd never heard him make a sound, I wondered what it would be. As I looked around, the war broke loose. He had a Gila monster nearly as big as he was and they were in a fight to the finish. He finally got ahold of the Gila monster at the back of the neck and broke his neck or shook him to death. He turned the Gila monster loose and it fell in the rocks limp. The little hairless, what I thought to be a worthless, dog had been bitten in the fight and whimpered faintly and fell over dead within three or four feet of the Gila monster. I realized you never know what's worthless.

I kept thinking that some of the Yaqui would pay me a visit because I knew they knew I was there. In a few days one walked into camp about noon and stayed long enough to eat some dinner and drink some coffee that I had bought from the old General at the commissary just in case I had company because I didn't drink it. He didn't have much to say and I stepped three or four steps away from the fire where I had some fresh water and when I looked around, guess he evaporated. He was gone.

In a few days another one came by a little older than him about the same time of day which made me think maybe I was camped a half day's walk from their headquarters. He had a little more to say, ate a little slower and took an extra cup or two of coffee, and when he left he shook hands and said, *"Mucho gracias."*

That night I was pondering that this second Yaqui didn't tell me about the wild horses. I guess I had been camped there about ten days when a whiteheaded old Yaqui walked into my camp while I was fixin' breakfast. He stayed to eat with me and had a little more conversation. He looked at my horses and began to tell me about a band of horses that were in the mountains and he waved his hand to the south the other side of their headquarters.

I showed as much interest as I could without attracting a whole lot of attention. He suggested that if I moved my horses to the south about two camps, I would be close to the wild horses he was talking about. After awhile he got up. He was a very straight thin little Indian and rather old but light on his feet and in good health He had delivered his counsel and advice and just walked off without saying anything else. I didn't let him get out of sight hardly until I began to put out the fire and clean up my camp and get ready to move.

It was up in the day before I got my horses packed and got my main herd pushed together and started up the mountain range in the direction he had waved his hand. Among the timber and the good grass, it was always easy to find a place to make camp. I didn't travel far that day and made a light camp that night so didn't unpack much. The next morning I got an early start. My horses were handling a lot better but it was still necessary at night to stake and hobble and keep a few horses handy around the water close to the camp and it always took a little bit of time to get them ready to travel.

I made a good drive that day. There were lots of floating clouds and soft mountain breezes and my horses traveled real good without showing much signs of the trip that night. I found some big boulders, bigger than lots of houses, and a nice big spring with plenty of tall shade trees and set up what I intended to be my permanent camp for a good while.

Next morning I saddled Beauty and started ridin' and huntin' for horses. This was still big country and even rougher to ride over and I didn't get very far very fast. I worked my way out towards the west edge of the high country hoping I would find some spots to scout from and see way off and save doing so much trackin' and trailin'. I hadn't had much luck and I decided in the early afternoon that I would start circling and try to get back to camp. I had been observant all day as to my direction and location of the sun and when the shadows were pretty long and I had begun to to wonder if I might spend the night away from camp because I was too dumb to find it, I saw a band of nice, fat, solid colored, good kind of horses in a little grassy spot at the bottom of a canyon. They were too far for me to get to them and get back that day but I sure was glad to know there was at least one band of wild horses in those mountains.

I turned Beauty in what I believed to be the right general direction, and as I had done many times before to give her a complete signal of what we were up against, I reached up and pulled her bridle off and tied it to the saddle horn. She knew when I did that that I was lost. She let her head down and ate a few bites of tall gramma grass and then raised her head and looked around and made about a half turn back to the right, the direction I had just come from and in a good straight steady walk without any looking back or looking around or showing any signs of human mix-up, climbed up over a point in the mountains and dropped back to the left about two hundred yards and I could see the spring in my camp four or five miles on the other side of the slope in front of us. I never apologized or pushed her or said a word and hoped she wouldn't tell anybody else when I was unsaddling her next to the spring.

I spent the next two or three days getting closer to this band of wild horses and began to see enough of them to know that they weren't branded and to know that they were sure enough mustangs. They were a little bigger and a little better quality in their feet and legs due to their mountain home than the ones I had caught in the Big Bend. It was about the third day that I waited by a place where they were watering on the creek with the wind blowing against me so that they wouldn't smell me until they came in to water. I was a little over anxious and as they began to turn back from drinking, I made a wild run into them and caught a nice fat mare that proved to have a little age on her and was sure mean to fight.

I had a four-strand silk manila lariat rope on her that she couldn't break, but she would run at my horse with her mouth open and we would have to dodge her and get her tangled up in the rope or she would turn back real quick again. I managed to get her wrapped around a tree and me to have the longest end of the rope and I got down and started to her head to put a hackamore on her. She was choking pretty bad and had rolled her eyes around and was watching me real close. In the split half second that it takes to slip the nosepiece over a horse's head is when she snapped my right hand. I pulled as quick as I could and she tore the skin about two and a half or three inches on the bottom and not quite that much with her top teeth, but I was jerking enough that she didn't bite a whole plug out of the back of my hand.

I decided there wasn't much point in worrying about whether she choked or not and I got on my horse. I was riding the big stout young bay horse that was green-broke when I left home and didn't mind putting some abuse on him, and me and him managed to wrap her some around that tree. I maneuvered my horse around and pitched the rope over her rump a time or two as I unwrapped her from that tree without giving her any slack. The choking for air had helped her disposition a little and she didn't make another run at us. All the other horses were clear out of sight and I drove, rather than dragged, this mare as much as I could and she was smart. She caught on pretty fast that dragging is when she choked and drive is when she could get her breath.

I got her to camp a little before dark and wrapped her around another tree and left the bay horse holding her. Then I saddled Beauty and roped and jerked her hind feet out from under which layed her on the ground straightened out. She already had me on notice that she was bad so I let them stretch and choke her while I put a hackamore on her and tied it to the tree. I slipped the lariat rope off of her head and got back away from her. Then I spoke to Beauty to step up and when she struggled to get up off the ground, she naturally kicked her back feet from the loop on that rope.

I had a fair smear of blood all over me and my clothes from this bite she had put on me and unsaddled both horses and went down to the spring and began to try to wash up. I didn't have any-thing much to doctor my hand with and I started to put a little bit of iodine on it. I realized there is no such thing as a little bit of iodine and knew it would burn those open gashes pretty bad so I washed it off good and greased it with a salty meat rind which has always been a good cowboy remedy. I thought to myself that in the clean high dry mountain air that it would probably get well without much doctoring. This was my roping hand and next morn-ing it was so swelled and stiff that I couldn't rope with it. I messed around camp and played with what gentle horses I had and walked by occasionally and kicked a little dirt at that old bay bitin' mare and didn't really care too much if she had broke her neck, but her kind don't have much bad happen to them.

About the third day my fist was about the size of a Texas grapefruit and I could barely stand to get my sleeve over it. The oldest of the whiteheaded Yaqui Indians came into camp that day, and I made a few signs and showed him my hand. He drew me a map on the ground with a small limb and marked a house and made enough signs and talked enough to make me understand that there was a doctor there. At least that's what I thought he said. I got on a horse and found the place in about three hours ride

88

and rode up to the yard gate of a little 'dobe hut and hollered hello.

There was a real old dried up Mexican woman, maybe part Indian, came to the door. She didn't speak but walked out to the crude rock fence that separated the yard from the rest of the world. I thought I would show her my hand and she would tell me where the doctor was. She looked at my hand and showed no sign of sympathy or asked how it happened or anything of the sort. She finally asked me if I had any white flour. I told her I did back in camp. Then she asked about some yeast, or at least I thought she meant yeast. I didn't have any yeast but had some sourdough that worked all the time in a jar that I carried with me to make sourdough biscuits. She told me to get the flour and the yeast.

I rode pretty straight and made good time because my hand had begun to hurt bad and red streaks were running up my arm from it. When I got back to her house, it was nearly dark and I thought she was going to do something right away to help my hand. She took the flour and the sourdough yeast and made sort of a wet paste out of it, not near as thick as dough. She poured this out on a flat rock and turned an old glass goblet with the stem broken off, making sure that this watery paste sealed around the glass. Then she told me three days from now that the medicine would be strong.

I wondered whether I would have a hand left in another three days but I laid around camp and bathed my hand in the spring and held it up to where it wouldn't throb quite so bad. The third morning I was at her 'dobe house by daylight. She waited until the sun came up and went out to the flat rock in her yard, and the goblet turned bottom side up had grown full of mold from the dough. She lifted the goblet and took her finger and wiped about a third of the dough and mold out from the glass and smeared it over the two raw reddish blue places on my hand. She made enough signs to make me understand that I would have to wait until nearly sundown and put it on again. I layed around under a big shade in her yard and she brought me some pretty hard kind of grub at noon and my arm began to get easy. My hand may not have been going down but it had quit swelling. She cleaned the place off good and doctored it again and wiped the rest of this mess up and wrapped it in a green dagger cactus leaf and said that would keep it moist. She told me to use it tomorrow and she would make some more medicine.

In about three days and the second goblet full of this treatment, my hand had gone down and there were protective scabs forming over the open places and I was able to go back to using my arm to handle a rope and work horses. Here was the making of penicillin in its first and crudest form and I was too dumb, as I guess thousands of other people had been, to recognize what the old medicine women knew would cure infection.

I offered to pay the old medicine woman, but she didn't want any money and said she could sure use some flour. I knew that these people lived on cornmeal because most of them raised their corn and they could rarely afford to buy white flour. I had bought some small sacks of flour at the commissary because I could pack them better than one big sack so the next day I took her a ten-pound sack of flour. She was sure happy to get the flour and made motions and signs and told me she would eat a little bit of it and keep the rest for medicine.

I managed to ride enough during the time that my hand was bad to keep my horses pretty well on a little range bordering up and down the stream and around the mountain that I was camped on. Next day I pushed them all in close to the camp and left them still loose and free to graze and started back to the canyon where I caught that last old bitin' mare. This band of horses weren't too badly scared from me catchin' that one mare and hadn't moved range.

As best I could tell there were about thirty head of mares and most of them had colts that had been born that spring. The stud was a seal-brown horse with a small star in its face and no white markings on his feet and a little bit larger than mustangs usually are. He didn't seem to have a whole lot of fear of one rider and he would put his mares in a protective spot but he had no fear of

coming out and meeting me which made me think he might be kin to that old mare I caught. There's no horse or nobody horseback anxious to have a fight with a range stud and this was making it pretty hard to figure out a way to get close enough to his mares to catch any of them.

I rode for several days moving these horses around but they always stayed in the foothills and never did get themselves in a bad spot where I'd have a chance to trap or rope one of them. I guess I had spent about a week at this kind of foolishness when one morning about daylight the old Yaqui Indian and two more about his age showed up at my camp before breakfast. I fixed them a big pot of coffee and fried them some flour tortillas and fed them on salt pork bacon and refried beans. When I about had breakfast ready, I thought I would make a hit with these old boys. I still had a few cans of cream corn that I had brought from the commissary so I poured it in on top of the beans while they were fryin' and stirred it all together. We had a few words along while I was fixin' breakfast and they sat by the fire and drank coffee.

That bunch of old chiefs sure did give that cream corn and fried beans a fit and bragged on the coffee but they weren't too fond of that old salty fat sowbelly, but they didn't have anything on me — I wasn't too fond of it either. They sat and smoked their pipes a little while, and I sat and watched them knowing if they had a proposition they would bring it up and it wouldn't do any good if I propositioned them anyway. After a while one of them spoke up and said, "One mare make you cripple. How you think you catch whole band?"

I thought that was funny and laughed and looked at my sore hand said, "I'm willing to learn from the Yaqui. Is there a better way to catch these horses?"

They sat in silence a while and I poured them some more coffee in their tin cups and directly one of them said. "Yaqui relay and trap horses and drive them into herd."

I said, "That sounds like good business for both of us."

They sat a while longer and the first old man that I had met said, "You pay."

And I said, "I don't know. How much?"

They sat a while longer and didn't say a word to each other and another one spoke up and said, "You pay one dollar a head."

I asked them, "How long will this take and how many horses are we talking about?"

The one that spoke the most English was the one that I had met the second time that came to camp by himself and he said, "One band of mares and one stud, maybeso thirty head."

I asked, "What about the colts?"

"Colts go with mares."

I asked them again, "How many days?"

They decided it would take ten, twelve maybe fifteen suns. I didn't trade with them right quick. I asked them if they had some young bucks that would take the job of herding the horses I already had and graze them around in the best places in the mountains. They studied about that awhile and one of them said, "Two, maybe three bucks."

I knew they had already counted my horses and knew how many there were and I nodded my head, yes. They said they would furnish three young bucks to herd the horses I had for $30 a month and I said that was too much money. They sat awhile and one of them said, "$30 for all three bucks."

I asked, "Would they ride some of the young horses while they herded them?"

One of them spoke up and said, "Yaqui no ride but break horses on foot."

All this conversation was broken Mexican, English, and Yaqui and it took a good many hand wavings and drawings of symbols in the dirt with a stick and the trade went on a long time. Long enough for them to drink another pot of black coffee. I finally told them it was a good trade for all of us and I would hire the three young bucks to herd horses and help keep my camp and I would trade with the chiefs for the band of mustangs at a dollar a head. Before they had time to get up, I asked did they want any money now. One of them said, "If we think you no pay, we no be here to trade."

With that they walked off. The next morning three lightweight young skinny Indian boys maybe seventeen or eighteen years old came into camp before breakfast. I wondered if I had traded to feed them while they worked but I didn't offer any argument because it looked like I had made a good trade even if I did feed them. I asked them if they had any breakfast and they nodded their heads that they had and I motioned to the coffeepot that I hadn't filled, and they all shook their heads, no. I began to make signs to tell them where the horses would probably be and wherever they took them to bring them back that night. While I was trying to get this over to them, one of them spoke up in very good English and said that they understood what I wanted done and that he had been to the white man's school and I didn't have to make signs nor worry about getting them to understand. He did say that the others didn't speak much English but he would tell them what I said. This sure was a relief to find a Texas-speakin' Indian that I wanted to herd horses and I could already tell that they didn't expect to eat at my camp.

I had found out that the Indian village was high up and on the south side of the mountain. I had been watching and knew that the band of horses hadn't been bothered. In a few days I rode over

94

to the Indian village and the old slender whiteheaded Indian was setting out in the sun when I thought it was the time of day to be shading up. He spoke to me and asked me to get down off my horse. Well, that was the first time I had been in their village and the first time I knew there would be any hospitality among the Indians. We sat on the ground a good while and said nothing till I thought I had been quiet long enough to be polite and I asked him about the horses. He said, "We move them now three days and three nights. They be tired and drove to your camp sometime."

I didn't know quite how to bring it up but I knew the horses hadn't been moved so I asked, "Where are you driving them?"

He said, "Better horses further west and more of them in band. Yaqui get more money and save little herd close to camp for later on."

I told him I needed *mucho* horses and that would be fine. I sat a little longer and I began to notice that their houses were all built of stone and seemed to be very old. I wasn't an Indian expert and I'm not one now but I had never been among Indians that had showed much signs or interest in the Christian religion. The only churches I had ever seen among the Indians in the western United States were those that had probably been built by the government or some do-gooders of different faiths. Well, setting in the center of the village nestled in this canyon in the high mountains was a very old stone church.

I said to the old chief that this was an old settled village and the Yaqui must not have been a wandering tribe. The old man was in his mellow years and glad to talk and boast of the heritage of the Yaqui. He told me that the Yaqui tribes were farmers and belonged in the valley of the Yaqui River. As early as the 17th century they had been converted by Jesuit missionaries and the church had always been the center of governing and social activities. He told me the Yaqui did not make war but had been at war with the Mexican government for nearly one hundred years and explained that hostilities might die down for eight or ten years at a time but the Yaqui never submitted to Mexican rule until after the 1900s and when they were driven into the mountains, they built permanent villages. As he talked, he pointed into a lower canyon where small children were waiting out the heat of the day with large flocks of sheep and goats, and said that they had learned to raise animals in the mountains instead of crops but they traded some with the Yaqui in the valley for what they couldn't raise such as corn and wheat and other foodstuffs. This was the most talking I had ever gotten a Yaqui to do and I sat quietly and didn't question or cross-examine him more than barely enough to keep him talking. I don't suppose any of this was too important to a horse wrangler and cowboy but the old man's way of telling it was fascinating and I could tell that he was a proud chief of a proud people.

That night I was settin' in camp thinkin' about what good shape I had my business in. I had three Indian boys herding my horses and another bunch relaying some wild horses and would finally worry them down to where they would drive into my herd for an awful good price per head. As I sat and looked in the fire, I wondered why I didn't pick out a town somewhere to go to for a few days. Next morning I talked to my English speaking Indian boy that I had named Palaver about how far it was to one of the better towns. He had never been to Chihuahua City but he knew that it was a long, long way. He had been to Hermosillo and said it was about three days walk. He never had been to Nogales but he had been told by other Yaqui that it was about the same distance. Well, when you go to figuring how far a day's walk is, don't you get the idea that a horse can do twice that far because those Yaqui will cover lots of country in a day and take all the short cuts.

I rode to the Indian village that morning and told the three old chiefs I was doing business with that things were going real good and it was still several days before they would have the horses run down and I needed to go to town for a few days. One of them told me that town was about four or five days ride on a horse or three days on foot. I asked him which town he meant, and he said, "Hermosillo."

I didn't really know the country too good but I didn't think it would be any further to Nogales and when I asked him about Nogales, he said the distance was about the same but Nogales was poisoned up with white man's ways. I guess he was forgetting I wasn't Indian and he thought it would be better to go the other way. I thanked him for his advice and told him if he missed me that was where I would be gone and would be back within seven or eight days. He watched me ride away but never did nod his head that he thought I should.

I rode in to Nogales in about three days leading one pack horse. I guess I was ridin' better horses than the Indians were talking about because I made it in about the same length of time as the Yaquis did afoot. I left my horses on the Mexico side of the border with a man at the customs station and went across the border into Arizona. I got a shave and a haircut in a barbershop and went to a cafe that had a sign in the window that said "AMERICAN FOOD." I had a big mess of sure enough pot roast, plenty of hot rolls and everything that went with it and topped it off with half of a apple pie and a double handful of ice cream which was the highest living I had done in a long, long time.

There wasn't too many unusual sights in Nogales, Arizona,

and in a way was more Mexican than it was American so I went back across the border in the middle of the afternoon and found a store where I could buy about the same kind of supplies as I would on the other side of the border. I put a good size pack on my pack horse and turned him and old Beauty back towards the mountains. I had been about three days riding to town. I had only spent the most of one day in town and with my pack horse well loaded, it would sure take another three hard days to be back in camp by the time I had told the old chief. Palaver had stayed in my camp to take care of things during the time I was gone and when I rode in in the night he got up and helped me unpack and unsaddle and gave me the news about what was going on, and sure enough, the outlaw band of mustangs were still being followed around on the range and weren't ready to be driven into the herd.

He had been gone from the village all the time that I had been gone to town so I thought I would send him home for a few days. I gave him a ten-pound sack of bean coffee and two five-pound sacks of white sugar and a dozen bars of Ivory soap. I had especially bought this stuff for the Indian village. He was all smiles and told me how the old men would like the coffee and the little ones would eat the sugar and the squaws would use the soap. I thought to myself that about covers the tribe.

He didn't stay gone from camp long and was back early the next morning with the word from the chiefs that the horses were getting closer to the part of the mountain range that we were herding my other horses and me and the young bucks should be ready for them in about two days. That strong coffee must have hurried up the horse business some. The third morning I waked up before daylight and heard a lot of horse talk and fightin' and nickerin' going on and the bucks must not have gone home that night because they had the whole herd of horses in a draw just

98

below the camp where we had been bringing them in to spend the night. I couldn't see them, but I could hear them and I knew there were some strange horses in the bunch.

The nights were always cold in the mountains and an outdoor man raises up and reaches for his hat and coat and puts his britches on in the morning under the cover if he has taken them off the night before. If he is sleeping out, he always puts his boots under the corner of the tarp where moisture won't get in them and make them hard to put on. I was dressed pretty quick and started to walk around one of those big boulders and noticed the fire was throwing its light way up the side of the boulder. When I got where I could see, there sat the three old chiefs smoking their pipes and waiting for a pot of coffee to boil.

I walked up to the fire and grunted at them about the same way they grunted at me, warmed a little bit and started fixin' some breakfast for all of us. They didn't say a word so I didn't either and as it got daylight, we could look off down in the canyon and see that there were some new horses and there was lots of nickerin' and squealin' and kickin' going on among my original herd and the new ones they had drove in late the afternoon before. I supposed it was late the afternoon before because Indians don't do much in the night. The old chiefs said, "Many horses. Much tired. Yaqui ready for dollar."

I made a few signs and asked how many dollars and the old slender whiteheaded Indian drew in the ashes at the edge of the fire "$32." I had the money on me but I went around the side of the boulder to my bedroll and shuffled around in the blankets while I managed to get the money out of my inside jacket pocket. I paid them in six $5 bills and two $1 bills. These old Indians showed a little humor and grunted and smiled and talked about how much money it was and one of them patted me on the shoulder and in

Indian told the others what I thought to mean "Good paleface."

Then I saddled a horse and rode down into the canyon among the herd and every horse that they had driven in was drawn and tired and you could ride up close enough to them to slap them on the rump with a bridle rein. Those Yaqui runners had relayed them day and night. You could also tell at a glance that my other horses had been grazing and weren't too interested in working what grass there was in the canyon and this bunch of new horses all had their heads to the ground eating whatever was in sight. I never knew that horses could be so exhausted by some breed of the human race following them on foot. The young Yaqui bucks were all smiles and the talkative one told me where there was one stud and he was much old and had his front teeth kicked out by some other wild horse and was not offering to fight anything in the herd.

This was catching thirty-two head of horses about as quick and cheap as I ever dreamed of and they were for sure wild because there wasn't brand, scar nor saddle mark on any one of them. Since we had no corrals and the Yaqui didn't work horseback, I wondered how they would manage to brand these horses for me. The bucks close herded the horses for several days and it seemed that they were not going to try to leave the herd but these horses made me uneasy because we hadn't staked or halter broke any of them and they were still chummin' up together and I thought that we should do something to break them up and mingle them through the herd.

Late one afternoon when they brought all the horses down into the canyon below camp for the night, we were settin' around the fire and the young bucks were drinking coffee before they set out to the Indian village. I thought it a good time to bring up the matter of branding the fresh wild horses and I wondered how we could do it. The least talkative one of the boys I think would have

100

been a horseman had it not been for his respect for the tribal tra-
dition of walking instead of riding. He finally said that we could
drive the horses all up in a close bunch and I could rope from a
horse the ones that needed branding and drag them out to the edge.
They would get some more Indians to help and they would pull
these horses down with ropes on their hind legs or by their tails.
That sounded to me like a pretty wild proposition and I wondered
how many extra Indians it was gonna take. We had had several
nice rains in the mountains and grass was extra good and holding
these horses up all day wouldn't hurt them much, but I didn't think
we could brand more than eight or ten a day the way he was talking about doing it. I told them to put out the word over at the
Indian village and find out which day we would have the most
help and we would try to brand the horses.

Well, I don't guess Indians have too heavy a schedule because
they were ready the next day and seven more bucks, some of them
maybe as much as forty years old, showed up with my horse
wranglers ready to fight these mustangs. They crowded the horses
up against the bluff on two sides and just kept them loose herded
on the other two sides afoot. They had learned to whittle out sticks
almost like walking canes, two or three feet longer, to use to
keep the horses back in the herd. We built a good fire and got my
brand hot that I had made out of a harness ring and I showed them
how they could pick it up with the horseshoeing tongs. I had my
doubts about how many horses would get away half branded and
how many Indians were going to get half killed.

I rode into the bunch and kept my loop down by the side of my
leg and real still until I got near a horse I wanted to catch. I never
spun my rope over my head or made any loose motion with it,
and good cowboys don't when they are working wild stock. The
only leverage I put on the rope was when I came up with it. I used

my wrist to throw it as fast as I possibly could and fit it on a horse. When that rope hit a mustang, bawlin', fightin', and chokin' started and dragging one any distance is real hard work on the rider and his horse. Before I had time to holler for help, one of my Indian horse wranglers was already there with a pole to encourage this pony to lead out of there right fast and we got them to the edge of the herd with less trouble than I had thought. This mustang had all four feet stuck deep under her and was pulling hard enough to be choking for air when one of the older Yaqui and about the heaviest bodied ran up and grabbed her tail and jerked it to one side and two more got hold and jerked her to the ground and hollered and made motions for me to keep pulling her. By now she was whistling real loud and these Yaqui may not know how to ride horses but they sure know how to hold one on the ground. They ran her tail between her legs and pulled it back up over her back and put their knees against her back and another one had gotten ahold of her head and was motioning for me to give her a little slack. He put both hands around her nose and clinched his hands together tight and pulled her head up in his lap and locked his legs around her neck. All of a sudden from somewhere came another Yaqui with that hot brand and branded her on the shoulder before she had time to hardly get her breath since I had given slack.

I changed horses several times during the day, not catching but four or five mustangs on the same horse until I would give him some rest. I told Palaver to explain to all of them that they were company so we would go up to my camp and fix dinner. Some of them grunted and talked around that there wasn't any use

As this stout Yaqui turned her head loose, he slipped the rope off of her and she got up and staggered a little bit and went back to the herd. This had all taken about twenty minutes and I could tell I had lots of help.

I changed horses several times during the day, not catching but four or five mustangs on the same horse until I would give him some rest. I told Palaver to explain to all of them that they were company so we would go up to my camp and fix dinner. Some of them grunted and talked around that there wasn't any use of eating until they got through. I sort of laughed at that and said that might be the Indian way but white men take a lot of pride in eating a regular meal. They all laughed and we went up to camp leaving three Indians to hold horses and later they came and ate. By middle of the afternoon we had branded all of the grown mares and all the colts and I told them that I didn't want my brand on that old stud — maybe I could manage to lose him when I started to drive out of the mountains.

For several days the bucks herded the horses and I rode around over the mountains hoping I might sight another band of mustangs and one time in the sleepy part of the day, I rode up on the three bucks setting on horses in the shade and thought I would tease them a little bit and said, " I didn't know Yaqui got on horses."

They all smiled and Palaver said that it was only the old ones that didn't ride horseback and the young ones didn't do it where it would be noticed by the tribe. I laughed and told them I didn't care if they all rode horseback — wished they did — we would get more horses handled that way. We moved the horses a few times in the mountains when some of the bucks would ride a horse part of the time. If a mare or a colt was about to leave the herd and go up the wrong way, they would jump off their horse and run afoot up through the rock to turn them back. This looked funny to me but it was the practical way for a Yaqui because he was so agile and fast afoot that he could skip across and head horses easier than he could putting a horse over rough terrain.

This was getting my new bought horses fat and used to being in the herd but it wasn't increasing my herd any and it was getting on up into the late summer. One morning when the bucks came to start the horses out to graze, I asked them if the Yaqui had sold me all the horses they wanted me to have or were the relay teams just resting up. Palaver said he didn't know, but he would ask the chiefs. In two or three days the chiefs showed up for coffee and breakfast. I waited around Indian fashion until the old white-headed one said, "You need more horses."

I didn't answer too fast but finally told him that I would buy that other band I knew about under the same terms. They sat awhile and smoked their pipes and finally spoke up that they would start that band in a little while. Well, I didn't know how long a little while was, but I knew if he knew he wouldn't tell me, so I explained that would be about all the horses I would want and it was getting late in the mountains. As it got cooler, I would like to push down into the desert and drive my herd into Arizona. None of them seemed to be interested in my plans or made any comment and I don't guess the weather bothered them one way or another since they were going to be there anyhow. In a few days I did see that they had started the herd and the relayers weren't getting very close to them. They were still fresh and were managing to catch a fast drink of water in the canyon they were used to. I supposed that the relayers would push them away from their native range before they really went to getting them where they could wear them down.

One day I was riding in the part of the mountains where the relayers were working and found a small girl maybe thirteen or fifteen years old sitting on a ledge under the shade of a tree with her things in a small *morral*. I tried to talk to her in English and I tried to talk to her in Mexican. She understood a little of my Mexican and I explained to her that she shouldn't be out there in the mountains by herself. She thought this was kind of funny and didn't know how to tell me what she was doing. I asked her to get up behind me on my horse and I would take her to the village. She wouldn't do that but she made signs that if I wanted her to go to the village she would trot along by my horse. The village was higher up in the mountains and where I was riding with my horse under a good deal of strain, this little Indian girl, who probably weighed less than ninety pounds, was trotting along at her own ease.

Of course, you never slip up on Indians and when we came into the village, the three old chiefs were setting out on a rock fence waiting for us. I explained to the old one that I had found this little girl off out there in the mountains by herself and was afraid that something might happen to her and that I had talked her into coming back to the village. The old chief smiled and by now two or three squaws were standing around. They giggled and it looked like everybody but me was well entertained and the little girl laughed and made signs with her hands. The old chief finally turned to me and said, "You no worry 'bout girls in the mountains. She one of team that relay horses. Rest of them girls too."

I tried not to show my amazement and then I laughed and waved my hand at the chief and the crowd that I didn't understand the ways of the Yaqui but I knew I couldn't improve on them. We talked on a little bit and the chief told me that the girls were lighter and faster afoot than the bucks and they don't get interested in trying to track a deer or watch some other wild animal and forget what they were supposed to do and that they had wore down that last bunch of horses and give them time and they would wear down this bunch. Everybody was amused by the whole incident and I, rather embarrassed, rode away from the village and left the Yaqui ways to the Yaqui.

The leaves had begun to turn on some of the trees in the high mountains and the nights were getting colder and Indian summer was almost on us. I guess them little Indian gals were a pretty fast bunch because they brought this band of horses in in about ten days. They pushed them into the other horses late one afternoon as the bucks were bringing the others into the canyon where we were holding them at night. There was a much younger and better looking stud and he and the old stud got into a big fight. All the herders and relayers climbed up on a high rock and stood and watched the stud fight like we would watch a prize fight. It was night before the young stud ran the old stud away.

I told my herders that night before they went to the village that if they could bring the extra help tomorrow, we would brand this twenty-seven head of new horses. As it seemed was the custom, the old one and his two other chiefs came to breakfast to be paid for running the horses into my herd. Before they got a chance to ask me for the money, I had it out in my hand. I paid them a $20 bill and a $5 bill and two $1s. They turned the $20 bill over and looked at it and passed it around among themselves and after their conversation, the old one turned to me and said, "This be enough money for next religious ceremony we have in fall."

After some gruntin' by themselves the old one turned and handed me a dollar bill and said it was for the old stud that I didn't want and they had charged me for. I tried to keep from taking it but I could tell that they would have considered it an insult to their honesty so I thanked them and put the dollar bill in my pocket with the remark that the Yaqui hadn't quite broke me and we all laughed. The chiefs stayed around and watched the fun while we branded horses that day.

Ever since I had moved up into the mountains and turned Yaqui, me and the rest of the tribe always had fresh deer meat. I furnished the rifle and bullets and Palaver or one of the other bucks kept the village in meat and when they killed a deer, they would bring me a hindquarter. We had fresh venison that we ate up that day at noon together with my other camp grub and everybody had a big time working the horses or watching.

106

It was early September and the weather had begun to change. In the high country they would have a rainy season in September. The old one said in a humorous way that I needed to move my horses and it would be better for a paleface not to lay out in the weather because I wasn't as tough as a Yaqui. He told me to bring my horses and move them into the village and they would graze my horses below the village until I was ready to go to Arizona. About all I needed to stay any longer for was to get hackamores and drag ropes on as many of these Yaqui horses as I could before starting them down into the desert. Any horse stepping on a drag rope will further his education and get his head and nose tender to where they are easier handled and they won't try to run away and leave the herd as long as something is dragging on them.

The next day we moved the horses up higher into the mountains on the west slope below the village and it took about all day. I led a pack horse up to the village and the old one showed me a shedded patio next to his house for me to unload my pack and camp in. He told me not to unpack my cookin' stuff. I would eat with him. We had supper about dark inside his house. This was the first Yaqui house I had been in. The walls were thick and the room was big with only one partition in the whole house. Most of the houses had oil skin or oil paper over the windows that could be rolled up or down, but there were no screens and very few glass windows except in the church. The old one being a chief had windows in the front room of his house and the back window had a very thin piece of buckskin, well oiled with all the hair taken off, that would let the light through and keep out the rain and cold. We sat awhile after supper and I got up and excused myself and went out to unfurl my bedroll and go to sleep. I was then and still am a light sleeper and have never been too well house broke, but after almost a year in the wild camping alone, it was kinda nice to be beddin' down where there was houses and good Yaqui people.

We started roping mustangs the next morning and putting hackamores on them and it took all the extra bucks that had been helping us brand and about three days to put all the hackamores and ropes that I had on these Yaqui horses. I realized that the grass wasn't as good near the village because of the flocks of sheep and goats that the children herded and my horses were spreading out every chance they could because of the lack of grazing. I rode in from the herd late one afternoon and my bedroll was scattered out over the rock fences. It looked like over half the village wash, but it wasn't. I had a few clothes wrapped up in my bedroll and they were getting awful ragged. My britches weren't as bad as my shirts because I wore leather chaps riding, but my shirts were torn and I had tied them together enough for them to hold on me.

I rode up and looked at my worn-out clothes and my clean blankets and the big duckin' sheet that was wrapped around the outside of my bedroll. They had all been washed and scrubbed but the first thing that bothered me was that I had a roll of money tied up in a piece of buckskin and I didn't know how to ask about my money without me hurtin' somebody's feelings. I was standing talking to the old one and told him that I was out of clothes which was another good reason that I needed to be pushin' on to Arizona before cold weather caught me when his squaw came up. She was a little bitty whiteheaded woman with a kind face and snarled crippled up hands and fingers. She said something to him and we walked over to where the rest of my camp riggin' was and she pointed over into a pile of ropes and there she had had thrown my roll of money. It hadn't been untied and had laid there all day and nobody had touched it. This helped my feelings considerably. I had lots of horses but that was all the money I had.

When I had first made camp in the mountains and they began

to furnish me deer meat, I had sent a whole slab of salt bacon to the village for two reasons. I damn sure didn't like to eat it and I thought maybe that the squaws would cook with it. They had no source of salt and they had chopped this up in very small pieces and divided it among themselves to use in cooking their beans and vegetables that they raised in small gardens. Well, I never felt like the squaws were obligated to me for a slab of salt bacon. They were actually doing me a favor to eat it up. The next day after the washing when I came in from working horses, the old one had a fresh new buckskin shirt that the squaws had made for me. They guessed pretty good because it was a good fit and I pulled it over my head and laced it up together in front. The old one said the squaws wanted to do this to repay me for the salt and the soap.

I had about all the ropes used up and all the horses haltered and they were spreading out hunting grass all the time so I packed all my riggin' one good afternoon and told the old one that I would like for the bucks to help me across the desert to the border. The old one said that would be all right and I could pay Palaver when we got to the border. He said they would send word to the Yaqui that lived in Arizona just across the border a little piece and south of Tucson and some of them could help me in Arizona. I didn't ask him how he would send word, but I felt sure that they would know I was coming.

When I had my pack horses ready and had Beauty saddled and was about to tell the old one goodby, he motioned to a little boy to come hold my horse and took me by the arm and started to the church. Several of the squaws that saw us and three bucks followed us into the church. I took my hat off and was as respectful as I knew how to be and didn't know what to expect. The inside of the church was well furnished and had glass windows and curtains made of handwoven wool. The woodwork was beautifully polished

and well kept and as the old one and the rest began to kneel, I kneeled too. I didn't understand a word they said but learned they were praying for my safe journey. I have never had anybody sell me any horses and then pray for my safe journey before or since. We walked back out to where my horses were and I shook hands with the old one and waved at the rest and hollered at the little kids and rode off.

Palaver and the bucks had the horses pretty well bunched and ready to string out down the mountains. We didn't stop to make any camp at dinner. It was real late afternoon and the sun was dropping behind the mountain to the west when we reached the foothills and Palaver helped me with fixin' supper. The Yaqui horses had pulled and jerked their heads all day because they hadn't quite learned how to travel by letting the drag rope drag over to one side and the whole herd was tired from the day's drive. I didn't think they would try to scatter in the night but it was good horse sense not to leave a mixed bunch of horses all night. So we guessed at the time in the night and changed guard and each of us rode about a third of the time slow and easy, not necessarily keeping the horses anywhere but just being sure they didn't make a run or start back into the mountains. They drifted and grazed some in the latter part of the night but in the beginning of the night they were real tired and mostly stood around on three legs or layed down.

Next morning we started driving about sunup and we were driving mostly west and a little north. In the early afternoon we maybe hadn't drifted over fifteen miles when we came to a pretty good hole of water in the desert that would water all the stock. It was too big a chance to pass that water at that time of day hoping to find water before night so the horses all watered and we made camp and sat around and rested ourselves the rest of the afternoon. We weren't in any hurry the next morning breaking camp and a Mexican rode up on a very sorry kind of little old stud with a hard, high, port bit on.

He was wearing typical spoke rowel spurs and the rest of the riggin' was a homemade Mexican saddle and a platted leather lariat rope. He said he had some horses to sell and if we would wait there till after dinner he would drive 'em to us. I asked him how many horses he had and he said twenty maybe thirty and pointed toward the west when I asked him where they were. We were going that direction and told him he could ride on back and meet us with his horses sometime tomorrow and explained to him the route we would be traveling. He asked how much I would give him for his horses and I told him I would have to see them and didn't promise him much about whether I would buy them or not. Palaver asked him detailed questions about a spring that would not be too far from his ranch where we could camp that night and he could bring his horses to the spring the next morning before we left. We had all this understood and Palaver had a pretty good understanding of the direction and how to get to the spring.

After he left and we were trailing the horses, Palaver rode up to me and said that if he understood him right he knew the spring and it would be about half a day's drive too far south from the way we were going but he didn't know whether there was any other water that we would run into. I told him I wasn't interested in losing half a day to get to buy any more Mexican horses and for him and the bucks to keep the horses pointed about the direction that we had all talked about in the village when the old one was telling us how to cross the desert.

Grass was good. The horses grazed and drifted easy. We weren't making very good time but I didn't know what difference that made. Time didn't mean much to an Indian or a horse and I had gotten to be enough Indian that it didn't mean much to me either. We found a dug earthen pool of water that was a pretty good size and there had been rain and it was full of fresh water. I knew that we were on somebody's ranch and that the ranch head-quarters must not be so awful far away, but in the desert water seems to belong to those that get to it. My horses actually didn't hurt the tank since it was full of fresh water and we made camp just under the dam in the shade of some cottonwood trees.

Before dark a rider came into camp. He was a man probably fifty years old and I could tell at a glance was a little more than a common cowboy. I introduced myself and shook hands with him and asked him to stay for supper. He said that this was his ranch and that his helpers had dug the pool in the early spring and it had been a good year and filled with water early. He was real proud of it. I told him that we would be careful not to damage the dam and try not to muddy up the water too much and I'd be glad to pay him for using the tank and pay him for the night. He studied a few minutes and asked, "Would five *pesos* be too much?"

I said, "That would be about $1.75 in American money."

I could see his face light up when I said American money and he said, "Si, señor."

I said, "In a case like that I'd be glad to pay you $2 and we'd both be happy."

I handed him two $1 bills and we shook hands. He got on his

horse and told me to stay and leave in the morning as late as I wanted to.

By sunup next morning I saw a swirl of dust coming across the desert. Palaver had seen it too and we figured it was our horse-sellin' friend so we waited around before we started our horses. to driftin' on west. He got to camp in about an hour from the time we spied his dust and his horses were wet with sweat and he had driven them hard since he hadn't run his bluff to get us to come by his spring. He had twenty-two head of decent kind of horses but a little on the thin side and I cut out ten head that I thought to be about three to five years old and could tell that some of them had been caught and handled and maybe rode some.

I told him I would give $3 in American dollars a head for these ten but that he would have to furnish me a *factura* because they were already branded. I was really worried about my Yaqui horses because I didn't have a *factura* for them. They weren't wearing anybody else's brand so I wasn't on dangerous ground from the standpoint of being accused of stealing them, but if I ran on to some *politico*, it would cost me more than a *factura* probably to bribe him into letting me keep them, and I began to want to get to the border pretty soon.

He waved both hands and went into a Mexican slobber and whipped himself with his hat and asked me $5 per head. I told him *adios* and told the boys to start the horses. About the time we were ready to leave, he took the $3 per head and we pushed the ten head into the tail end of the herd and as hard as he had driven them, they were going to have trouble keeping up. I asked him about the *factura* and he was ready. He had one in his pocket already made out for twenty-two head and I paid him $30 in cash for the ten head and stuck the *factura* in my pocket thinking to

114

myself that I had enough to cover twelve more head but it still wasn't near enough.

We found a little desert ditch with a small stream of water running in it a little while after high noon. We hadn't come very far but I was afraid to pass it up and take the chance of making a dry camp so we started to turn the horses into a mill and get them stopped from driftin' and picked out some little scrawny mesquite trees to make camp under. As the horses milled around and drank, some of them went further up stream, maybe a quarter of a mile, and the oldest buck rode up to turn them back. He came back and told us there was a big blue water hole up there and it would be a lot better water for us to drink and a better camp site. We hadn't quite made camp and moved on up to this better water and better shade.

The desert was a lot hotter than we had been used to and all our horses were sweating a lot more and quitting early in the day on good water and shade was gonna be better for my stock and for us too. We had camp well spread out and had hung cookin' vessels and stuff around on limbs and it looked like we might be staying a few days which wasn't my intention. I had sat down on the ground and leaned back on my bedroll when I saw a rattle-snake about a hundred feet from camp. I hollered at the boys and they rushed over. One got him to coil where he wouldn't be trav-eling off and another cut a mesquite limb where it had a fork in it and stuck it down on the back of the snake's head holding it to the ground. The other buck got brave when the snake's head was staked to the ground and uncoiled him and put his foot down on him about middle ways toward his tail. He hurried around camp and finally got the horseshoeing tongs and as the snake jobbed his fangs out, they would try to catch them with the tongs and finally did. Everybody was working with great excitement and were being careful to not break the fangs off but were trying to pull them out.

In the beginning of this episode I had told them to kill the damn snake. They grunted a few times in a tone that I could well understand that my idea didn't suit them. They caught a horse, and pulled eight long hairs out of his tail and in a matter of seconds had rolled and twisted them together and made a cord. They made several half hitches around the snake's body with the horse hair leaving just enough room to tie it to the end of a rawhide string. Since they had pulled the snake's fangs out, I decided I wouldn't interfere but find out what the Yaqui way was of dealing with a rattlesnake. They tied this rawhide string to the bottom of a small mesquite bush. Then they took the stick off and backed off all at once. They laughed and talked among themselves and was real proud of each other. When they got their breath, I asked Palaver, "What in the hell are you doing? Do you aim to start a snake ranch and you're mustangin' you some stock?"

He laughed big and told the others and they had a big laugh too. Then he said, "Snakes are evil spirits of bad Mexicans and this one will change the tune of his rattlers and call many snakes to come and get him loose."

I said, "Hell, one snake's enough. What do you want to call any more for?"

He said, "It's early and long time before sundown. Snakes hear his sad tone and he thinks they come to get him loose and they don't. They come to kill him at sundown. Then we kill many bad spirits of Mexicans that have bothered Yaqui."

I said, "Well, I hadn't intended to get into the Mexican-Yaqui war but I guess this will be my part of it."

It wasn't long until we could hear snakes up and down the

grass around that branch of water answering each other. Well, I couldn't set down any longer and I damn sure wasn't fixin' to take a nap so I stood around in the shade where I could turn around and watch everything that might be crawling. Palaver said it would be best if we all stayed in the same place so they moved over with me. This to me was the most horrible experience that I ever had outdoors and I have killed all sorts of wild animals but to stand there and wait for a rattlesnake reunion was a little hard on my unsettled nerves.

This wasn't a big snake, probably two and a half feet long, and the first two that crawled out of the grass to him were about his same size. They crawled up by him and over him. Then came some smaller snakes — I guess just one crop later. I was anxious to kill them as they came up but Palaver said they would smell the smell of death and the rest of them wouldn't come. Well, about as long as my nerves could stand it and just before sundown, we counted six that had come up to kill that snake and they may have been waiting for sundown but I told Palaver that was going to be too long for me. I wanted them killed while there was still plenty of light so they took sticks and rocks and fought and beat those snakes to death. I offered them my rifle but Palaver said they would get more good out of the evil spirits from the bad Mexicans beating them than they would shooting them. When these snakes were sure enough dead and their heads beat to a pulp, they cut their rattlers off and carried the snakes about a hundred yards from camp and threw them on a pile of rocks.

This snake roundup sure fixed my nerves and everything I saw in the way of leather or rope I thought was crawling. The bucks came back and sat down and all talked about what a great thing it was to have killed the evil spirits of the Mexicans and now we could camp there as long as we wanted to because all the snakes were gone. Well, I had trouble staying there the rest of the night and I sure wasn't going to camp there any longer because I didn't know but what those snakes had a grapevine system like the Indians and there were more coming.

Next morning when we were fixin' breakfast, the bucks walked out to the pile of rocks to be sure there wasn't any more snakes come up in the night. They came back in a few minutes well satisfied that they had destroyed a whole family of them. We broke camp and saddled up and started drifting horses a little after sunup. The horses had grazed on some good grass along the branch that night and had plenty of water and they started out traveling real good and I thought we might take up some slack from the short trip.

After the horses sort of had the fresh worked off of them and settled down to driftin', just for fun these bucks would ease in the bunch and pick up a halter rope and scuffle around and get on one of these mustangs. Sometimes they would buck real quick and sometimes they would run away, but whatever the catch was, whether they were thrown or stepped off, these young Yaqui bucks always landed on their feet and they seemed to have a big time playing with the horses. Once in a while one would say he believed he would let his feet rest and would pick out a horse he knew would ride and just catch him by the halter rope and jump on him. If they needed to head the horses to turn them one way or another they would jump off that horse and run afoot to turn the herd. All of this kind of foolishness kept the drive from being monotonous and now and then one of them would get thrown over a horse's head or something to add to the day's fun.

We ate cold grub for dinner that we cooked at breakfast instead of stopping for a noon camp. Palaver thought he knew where there was water on our trail due south of Nogales. We found this stream in late afternoon just a little before sundown. We had drifted the horses hard all day and were ready to water and rest and camp. Nogales was a port of entry for livestock coming from Mexico and this watering that we camped on must have been pretty well used because the grass was grazed short and scarce close to the water. We took time that night holding the horses after they got rested and began driftin' to hunt better grass.

We broke camp next morning and I told the bucks to drift these horses just far enough south to get into better grazing and then hold them up and wait for me cause I was going to ride into Nogales to see about some business and would catch up with the herd the next day. It was no great distance to Nogales and I rode in a little before noon. I rode up to the port of entry and asked if I could ride my saddle horse into Arizona. The Mexican official at the gate told me that the entry on horses was $15 a head and if I was going to ride over into Nogales, Arizona, I would have to put up $15 and get it refunded if I came back within three days. I laughed and said it wasn't far to walk and it wasn't. It was just through the gate where we were talking. I told him I would leave my horse in Mexico and come back later in the day.

There was no fee for a man to cross afoot if he identified himself as an American citizen going and coming. I didn't have a lot of time to spare because the longer I fooled around in town the farther the herd would be away from me. It was still wise that I had them drift the herd to where there was something to eat even if I had decided to come across at Nogales — we would just be backtracking for a few days grazing. I had a big cafe dinner and crossed back over the border and got my horse. After I got out of town, I took a southwesterly direction and started hunting my herd. Along the border there were a good many small ranches that I rode past but I didn't bother to ask any questions because I hoped they hadn't seen my horses or knew anything about them. I finally

119

struck a plain trail and could tell it was my band of horses because I had ridden the little strawberry roan and my other saddle horses were shod and I could clearly pick out Beauty's tracks and the young bay horse's tracks. It wasn't a bright moonlight night but it was clear and open enough to see tracks and so I rode on and found camp a little while before midnight.

We figured that we were maybe twenty miles west of a direct line from Nogales and would be west of Tucson and pretty close in line with the Yaqui village that was between Tucson and the border so next morning we pointed them north and about middle of the afternoon we rode onto the border. The border of the United States and Mexico along the American line in those days was marked about every five miles with what looked kind of like a sharp pointed tombstone about four feet high. We bunched the horses up in a good tight bunch and we had been driving the pack horses all this trip, and I was sure they were in the middle. There wasn't any sign or sight of people as far as the eye could see so all of a sudden we backed up from the north side of the herd, hollered and squalled a few times and sure enough that bunch of horses stampeded across the Arizona line and we weren't able to head them for about five miles.

The horses were tired and grass was good but there wasn't any water in sight and I felt like they would like to stop to graze. They had watered good twice that day and I probably wouldn't have any trouble with them until tomorrow. All the horses that we had hackamores and drag ropes on had gotten real easy to herd and handle and had learned to carry their heads sideways so they wouldn't step on their drag ropes too much.

By now it was almost dark and these young bucks were afraid to stay on the wrong side of the border all night. I owed them for a week's work which would be about $8 so I gave them a $10 bill

120

to give to the old chiefs and a $5 bill apiece to keep for their own because they had done me such a good job and we shook hands in the night as they left afoot to go back to the mountains.

I didn't unpack much that night except my bedroll and I kinda reached through my pack and picked out cold grub. The night that I rode in late from Nogales, the bucks had used up a lot of their time cooking the kind of grub they could carry to make their trip back to the mountains when they left me. So that night I had plenty of cold grub to eat without making camp. They had plenty of cooked beans that they had dried and we had cooked up all the fresh meat we had left and they had made tortillas that they would use for bread. The bucks had unpacked the pack horses before they left and about all I had to do was unfurl my bedroll and go to sleep.

About daybreak the next morning I heard my horses moving around some and raised up and looked around but saw nothing was bothering them. I talked a little bit to old Beauty and she came up out of a draw where she had probably grazed most of the night. Before I started breakfast I saddled her and left her reins loose to graze with the bits out of her mouth but where we could get started quick if we had to. I heard a low whistle off in the distance that I knew was some form of human so I whistled a little bit myself and cleared my throat. I could see a man walking out the other side of the most of my horses. I raised my voice enough for him to hear me but without scaring any horses and told him to come on into camp.

This was another Yaqui, probably about fifty years old, dressed in pretty good American cowboy clothes but wearing regular Yaqui shoes. We shook hands and he spoke good English and told me that he had word from the old one that I would need some help, and there were three others that had gone around my horses and were bunching them and bringing them back towards us. We visited awhile and I told him that I wanted to strike a trail north that would lead me west of Tucson. He said that he and his friends knew the country well and would help me along with my horses but he laughed and told that the Yaqui blood had got thin north of the border and him and his friends would want to ride. I said that was fine. I had plenty of horses and bridles but no saddles except those that I was using for pack. He told me that they had thought as much and had brought saddles with them.

I thought to myself that I was talking to a Arizona Indian instead of a Yaqui mountain Indian and I had better find out about the money. I asked him how much a day they would expect for helping me and he said all four could go with me up as far as Phoenix if I was going that direction and that they would want $1.50 a day apiece. I knew that I would be getting into ranches and fenced country and maybe have to follow roads some and would need their help bad so we made a trade without any trouble. I also knew that I would have to feed these hands since we would be moving and they wouldn't be near their settlement.

By now the others had walked the horses up into a fairly tight herd and they were all seasoned grown men that had been working on ranches in Southern Arizona off and on most of their lives. I slipped the bit in Beauty's mouth and rode into the horses and roped out some of the Knoches Bros. horses that I knew would ride. This wasn't going to be too bad a deal because I was fixin' to get eight or ten horses a day used and schooled a little more than they were. They told me that if we followed the arroyo about twenty miles, we could camp on good water. This was the first time in a long time I had heard an Indian describe distance as miles instead of days, and I could tell that my expenses were going up but my trip was going to be easier on me, I thought.

We drifted the horses nearly all day and I let the Yaqui kinda

122

pick our trail and that night we camped south of Twin Butte on a pretty good mountain spring. We had crossed desert country all day. Greasewood and catclaw and scrawny mesquite covered the earth as far as we could see and there was very little grass. The horses traveled slow and did their best to graze out a fair day's fill. The next afternoon late we camped in sight of the old San Xavier Mission. The water was pretty bad in this little draw and the horses didn't water too good and hadn't grazed too good. Of course the Indians didn't notice that but I intended to try to keep these horses going good until I found a place to sell 'em or load 'em on the railroad.

We fixed a pretty good supper and since these Arizona Yaquis spoke and understood English, we had got pretty well acquainted. After supper, maybe not the oldest but the grayest Yaqui said he would like to go up to the mission and visit and would be back by bedtime. One of the others said he didn't think the horses were going to be any trouble that night and believed he would go with him. Of course, I chimed up and said, "Boys, I haven't known you too long but I imagine that being cowboys, it wouldn't hurt you to go up there and do a little confessin' on the side."

I don't know what time they came into camp that night, but very early the next morning one of the Fathers walked down to the camp at a very appropriate time to get breakfast and drink coffee while he visited with everybody. I was nice as I knew how to be to a man of the cloth, but I didn't intend for him to interfere too much with my day's work. When he saw I was getting ready to go ahead and start my horses and move camp, he said that the mission was in need of a gentle horse to work to a light cart. He thought I might have one that I would donate to the cause. I told him I had worked a year for these horses and I hadn't sold any or took in any money in trade and I wouldn't be too inclined to help

123

the cause. Well, he thought that we ought to pray over the matter and he had great faith in prayer. I told him I knew he must have great faith, but I didn't believe he could pray me out of a horse. He finally laughed and said, "Well, we have some mules and burros at the mission and we'll trade a mule for a young horse."

I pointed out one of the horses that I had bought from the Mexican and told the older Yaqui to lead him to the mission and bring back the mule. I didn't go look at the mule and didn't think I could be too bad cheated on a $3 horse even by the Father. By now, I had named the greyheaded Yaqui, Chief, because he was the one that did the trading and talking. Chief brought back a little bitty, mossy-headed, sweeny-shouldered, dun mule with a stripe down his back that had seen every bit of thirty winters and was so gimpy in his foreshoulders that he would not do to ride, work nor pack and I thought to myself, it is possible to get cheated even on a $3 horse.

We had tied the little mule up for the night and the next morning when we started to move camp, I knew he wouldn't be able to keep up with the drive so I turned him loose. He dropped behind the herd and I watched him go back to the mission and just thought, there might be something to that praying business Father had talked about because he had both my horse and his mule.

We drifted the horses up the canyon and still didn't run into any fences and found a little better camping place on Brawley Wash late that afternoon and and had better water. Brawley Wash was just due west of Tucson and about two or three hours ride. I left the Indians to ride green horses and loose herd while I rode into Tucson next day. I went around the stockyards and a few horse lots but traders were out of money and had lots of horses and nobody was much interested in my horses. Some offered to come

124

out and look at my band of horses and maybe trade me something, but I could tell it was a broke situation and their horses wouldn't be as fresh looking stock as what I had, so I went downtown and bought me a fresh change of clothes and went by a hardware store and bought enough horseshoes and nails to shoe ten head of horses all the way around. We put them in a feed sack and tied it on the back of my saddle and I started back west to the herd.

We moved across the Papago Indian Reservation for several days and made two dry camps, but this was my way of staying out of fence trouble and staying away from roads. We camped one night at Bitter Wells and the next night at Johnson Wells and as we started north we ran along the foothills of the Maricopa Mountains where the grass was good and my horses filled up. In a few more days we were on the west edge of the White Tank Mountains and had found water on the Hassayampa River northwest of Phoenix. We had crossed somebody's fence during the day and had done a good job of letting it down and driving the horses over it and putting the fence back up and tying it real good, and up to now nobody had ridden in to my herd to say anything about us crossing the country.

I told Chief that I remembered they wanted to quit at Phoenix, but I wanted them to stay on long enough to shoe some horses and let me go to town and when I came back I would pay 'em and they could turn back. Chief grinned pretty big and said, "We thought we try you a little. We see you pretty good fellow and feed good, so we no quit."

I said, "Well, that's fine. We'll just keep driving further north when I get back."

It was a hard day's ride from where we were camped on the Hassayampa River to Phoenix but I thought there might be some horse business in Phoenix so I left the Indian hands to shoe ten head of horses with the shoes I got in Tucson while I rode into Phoenix. I had been making it a practice to rest Beauty as much as I could and save her for times where there would be trouble so I took the strawberry roan on my trip to Phoenix.

I got there late in the afternoon and rode into one of those dude horse renting places and asked if I could put my horse up for the night. This fellow had about twenty-five head of rent horses, and in the rent horse business around a winter resort, it takes a man with more patience to take care of them duded than it does high quality horseflesh and his bunch looked pretty hard. He half apologized to me about the kind of horses he had but he said they were the kind he needed to take care of snowbirds that came down here from the north to spend the winter in Phoenix and decide to go western and come rent a horse that they think they might be able to run to death and he was very careful not to have any that they could harm.

He took me uptown in his pickup and on the way I asked him about the possibility of me selling some horses and told him what kind I had and where they were. He said he doubted if there was anybody in the horse business around town that had any fresh money to buy stock with but he imagined I could strike up a trade with a competitor that had sorrier horses than he had. I thanked him for this information and told him I would see him the next morning when I came after my horse.

I got a room at a hotel and took a bath with hot water for a change. That night I was eating supper in a cafe just far enough from the hotel that there would be a difference in the price of the grub. There was a light complexioned Swede fellow, pretty big boned and big mouthed, came in and sat down at the counter close to me. He gave the waitresses a hard time and they seemed to know him and didn't pay him much mind. I was done eating when he

126

struck up a conversation and told me that he had a riding stable out on Indian School Road which was a way out of town. He started in to telling me what good horses he had and how much business he did and that the winter guests just about kept his horses rode down business was so good.

I told him I was in the horse business too and had a pretty good herd of horses camped about a day's ride west of town and if he needed any fresh stock, I would be glad to sell him some. Well, his conversation just brightened up like he could buy the whole bunch and said he would ride out the next day to look at them. Later he changed that "ride out" part and said he would come out in his station wagon after I had had time to get back to my camp. I explained to him about where I was and he said he knew all the country and had took trail ride parties all up and down that river.

I caught a taxi to take me out to where my horse was the next morning and this fellow had fed and brushed and cleaned the strawberry roan off and had him ready for a day's work. While I was saddling up I told him about my horse buyer and he told me more about him than I had told him and said if I did any business with him to be sure and get my money first and not to trade for any horses because the bank had a mortgage on all of them and maybe some that were already gone. Well, it looked to me like Phoenix was another dead deal so far as the horse business was concerned.

I got back to camp about three o'clock in the afternoon and my big blistery-lipped horse buyer was already there. He had picked out sixteen head and most of them were from the Knoches Bros. horses and a few Yaqui horses. We weren't long tradin' at $25 a head which would be $400. He said that since he had come out in his station wagon I would have to drive and deliver them back to Phoenix for him. Well, that didn't mount to no big thing so

I told him we could bring them in tomorrow. Well, he was about to get in his station wagon and go back to his hurry-up horse business when I said, "I'll have to have the money for 'em before I drive 'em to town."

He spluttered and got about half mad and half smart and said that there wasn't any question about the money. He just wanted the horses delivered when he paid for them and I said, "There is a question about the money because I want it before I deliver 'em."

He got pretty huffy and said, "It sounds like you don't think I have $400."

I said, "No, I didn't say that. I just said I wanted $400 before I go to the trouble of drivin' sixteen head of horses to Phoenix, but since you've gone to the trouble to come out and get your feelin's hurt, you can pay me $200 now and $200 tomorrow when I get 'em to town."

He blowed off some more steam and said that horses were hard to sell and he knew I wasn't going to pass up a chance to sell sixteen head to one buyer and he'd be looking for us to drive them in tomorrow. I said, "Well, if you look too hard, you're liable to be squint-eyed cause I sure ain't comin'," and with that he kicked up a batch of dust in that station wagon and left camp.

I turned north on purpose into Wickenburg and found a set of stockpens to put my horses in and bought enough alfalfa hay to feed a couple of days hoping I might have some trading business. Wickenburg was a pretty good size Arizona town of maybe a thousand or more and I had a few lookers but nobody wanted to pay money for any horses. While we were camped in these stock pens, I took advantage of the use of the chute to put my brand on that last ten head of horses that I had bought from the Mexican. One of these Yaqui men had turned out to be a pretty good cook and we were close to town where we could buy meat and some other stuff that we weren't used to, so we had a feast for a few days, but I had begun to worry about my money and was trying pretty hard to do some horse business.

There was a whiteheaded old cowboy came down to the stock pens one day and walked through my horses and visited, drank a cup of coffee and said he would like to have a good young horse

but all he had to trade for it would be a heifer calf. Well, I didn't rightly know what I would do with a heifer but I knew that a calf was worth more than a horse right then so I asked him some questions about his calf. He said he lived out in the edge of town on the creek and he had a jersey milk cow that had a half Hereford calf and he sure needed a ridin' horse.

I was settin' by the fire on my bedroll and told him to look through the horses and pick out one that would suit him. Directly he hollered and was pointing his finger around. I walked out in the bunch and he had picked out one of the Mexican's horses I had bought. He wondered if I he could catch him and look in his mouth. I could tell he was sure enough an old stocker so Chief handed him a rope and he slipped his loop over that fresh branded horse's head and they scuffled around a little bit before he got up to him and got his hands on him. He had a four-year-old mouth and was a fairly decent kind of Mexican horse.

I told him that I'd saddle a horse and ride out to his place and look at his calf. I knew somebody would buy a calf and I'd turn it into money. I rode my horse in a walk and the old man walked along beside. We visited and it wasn't far out to his place and he had a good fat heifer calf that would weigh about four hundred pounds. I would be cheating him bad so I thought I'd better test him to see if he thought he ought to draw any boot. I questioned him and asked him how much boot would he give between the heifer and the horse he picked out which gave him a chance to proposition me if he had any boot in mind. He said, "I can't pay no boot, but I sure do need that pony. I've staked this calf out and it's gentle to lead or to drive and you could maybe sell it here in town."

I said, "Well, I guess it's a fair enough trade," and handed him a lariat rope and said, "Why don't you just lead the calf afoot back to the stock pens."

He said, "Yeah, that won't be no trouble," so I tagged along behind while he led the calf.

He had brought a halter rope with him and I loaned him a rope and he caught the horse he wanted and got a halter on him and said, "I wonder if he'll ride bareback."

"I don't know," I said, "but there's one way to find out."

He knew what that was so he jumped up on him. This old pony kinda goaded a little bit with him but didn't actually buck and he got his head pulled up and the Yaqui cook that I was calling Tortilla opened the gate and led him out in the road. This horse hadn't been rode much and I saw him leaning over slapping him on one side of his jaw or the other to turn him the way he wanted to go. Chief spoke up and said, "You think maybe we camp here long enough to eat up that calf."

I said, "No. We'd have to buy flour to go with it and our money would run out."

Everybody kind of laughed, but they didn't really know whether I was tellin' the truth or not.

Next morning we was about to feed up our last alfalfa and I started around hunting a cow buyer to sell my calf to. Up in the middle of the morning, I run on to the old cowboy I traded with and told him I hadn't found anybody to buy that calf. He told me he couldn't either and he couldn't ship just one head so he was glad to trade her off. I went to the local meat market and he said that he was killing some of his own cattle and wasn't buying any outside stock. I asked him that if I could sell the calf, about what was it worth. He said maybe a nickel a pound on hoof and I thought to myself, I still wasn't hurtin'. It would be good trade if I could get $20 for the heifer. We was havin' dinner in camp and a fellow rode up and hollered that he heered I had a heifer for sale, and I said, "Sure do. Get down and have some dinner and we'll talk about it."

He was like everybody else in the stock business along about then, if he made his dinner, it would have been a pretty good day's work so he tied his horse and came over and got a tin plate. I believe he could put more grub on one plate than anybody that ever eat with us. The heifer was standing among the horses and while we ate, we talked. He said he was a little short on money and was trying to start him a cow herd. He had some horses and since I was more in the horse business than the cow business, he believed I ought to trade with him for a horse. I said, "Well, I like to change colors. What kind of a horse have you got?"

He said, "A good little brown Mexican horse that's just green-broke. I traded a older gentle horse for him yesterday."

I said, "Before I go look, there has to be some boot change hands between that good heifer and a Mexican horse."

He said, "Well, I might give a little boot because I need cows worse than I do horses."

I asked, "Where's your horse?" And he said, "He's out here pretty close. I'll lead him down here directly and you can take a look at him."

Directly he came up leading the Mexican horse that I had swapped for the heifer. I told him it was a decent enough little horse but not enough for that heifer. I'd have to have $10 boot. He said there wasn't $10 difference in nothin' that walked on four feet but he would give $5. Well, that's an old trader's trick. I knew he was trying to split the difference and I said, "Well, I'll flip a half dollar out in the dust with you that you pay me $5 or $10.

He said, "I ain't a gamblin' man, but I'll split the difference with you and pay $7.50."

I said, "That ain't enough, but that heifer ain't goin' to travel too good with these horses so turn the horse loose and drop your twine on that heifer after you pay me the difference."

He counted out five $1 bills and five half dollars which I guess was about all the money he had and went off leadin' the heifer. This $7.50 was the first money that I had took in in the horse business in a year and I thought maybe my luck was changing.

The horses and the Indians and me were well rested and well fed and I thought I would drift still further north up into the territory west of Prescott. I ran into some trouble with ranchers about crossing so many horses on their land and every chance I got to camp in somebody's small pasture with water I would pay for two or three days' grazing and camping rights to keep from having to herd all the time.

There were a good many Indians came to us and a few ranchers when we camped on the Santa Maria River about forty miles west of Prescott, but nobody offered to buy or even trade for any Mexican or Indian horses. We had a pretty bad electric storm one night and a bunch of horses ran over a barbwire fence and some of them got cut up pretty bad. A Charley Green filly was cut up so bad that when we drifted out, we left her on the river because she couldn't travel. We were in higher country and mostly crossing an Indian reservation and the grass was better but the country was awful dry and water was real scarce. We made a dry camp one night after we left the Santa Maria River and the next night we camped on Burro Creek west of a settlement called Camp Wood. This was a little different kind of water and two of the horses that had been ridden most of the day took water founder that night and couldn't travel. I kept having the Yaquis change horses twice a day and they had begun to ride some of the young mares that I had been letting drag halter ropes all this time that came from the Yaqui horses out of the mountains.

We drifted north along the foothills of the mountains hoping to find water. Mountains mean water if there is any, and I thought maybe it would be better to work up into the high country but it was easier driftin' our horses in the foothills. We stomped down a fence along the middle of the morning and drove the horses over it. We were always careful to put these fences back up in good shape, but it seemed like that morning my luck had run out. A unhappy character rode into the herd and began hollering at me wanting to know who owned the horses. I told him I did. He said, "You got a lot of nerve to be crossin' this country without nobody knowin' it."

And I said, "Well, since don't anybody know it, seems like you might be part Indian and got a smoke signal from somewhere."

Of course this rubbed him the wrong way which didn't bother me none because he hadn't started out to be nice or try to get along with anybody. He was packing a saddle rifle and I was too, and he jumped me about my rifle and asked, "Don't you know it's against the law to carry a rifle in a national forest reservation?"

I said, "Then looks like we're both guilty."

"Don't be so smart with me. I've got a forest grazing permit and you haven't, or if you do you're a way off of your territory."

Two of the Yaqui were listening and I could tell that they didn't like the situation. He said, "I'll find somebody with enough authority to take care of you."

"Well," I said, "I hope they know how to take care of horses too," and he rode off in a pretty fair lope.

We made camp for dinner and had found a little water, enough

134

to water on but not enough to camp and stay on. We ate dinner and moved on further up the country. About middle of the afternoon this one man unwelcomin' party rode back into the herd and had a forest ranger with him. The forest ranger said that he would have to hold the horses up and go back to his station while he found out what to do with me. We were in a good grassy spot and high enough up that there were a few little lakes around with snow water in them. I told the boys that if I wasn't back by dark to make camp and take care of the stock.

We rode about ten miles back down toward Camp Wood to a forest ranger camp. The ranger got out a grinding telephone and talked somewhere and told them about the situation. During this time this rancher was passing little pleasant remarks to me asking questions that I didn't seem to be able to find the answers for right handy until we was both just settin' lookin' at each other like two mad bulls that didn't want to fight because the weather was too hot. After three or four of these grinding phone messages, the ranger wasn't exactly happy to be in this situation, but he was trying to handle it in a businesslike manner. He said, "It might be that I could get you off if you would pay pastureage for the time you are on the forest reservation."

I didn't know a whole lot about these forest grazing permits but did know enough to know that they were awful cheap and they didn't charge much per head per year for a man to get a permit to move up in the forest and spend the summer with his livestock.

I asked, "Well, at $2 a head a year how much do you figure three days grazin' would be worth on one hundred and forty head of horses?"

The rancher spoke up and said, "That's goin' to get into too much figurin'. Why don't you just fine him aplenty and have him move on out?"

The ranger was trying to be legal and said, "I don't think I have the authority to fine a person. That would take somebody above me."

I didn't know who he was talking about and said, "Well, the longer you worry about me and the more you do to me, the more of that high country grass my horses are going to eat so just take all the time you want to. If I ain't under arrest, I'm going back to camp."

Mr. Forest Ranger said, "Don't you move your herd of horses from where you are until you contact me again."

This old rancher begun to bust up after I mentioned grazing these horses. It didn't seem to dawn on him until now that he would have been better off to go ahead and let me get out of the country. Mr. Forest Ranger said that since this had been brought to his attention and he had called a higher authority, he would have to have instructions from them before he could make a settlement in the case.

I said, "That's fine. Me and my stock and hands need the rest."

I left in a pleasant mood but I could hear that rancher talking in higher tones of voice and getting more nervous as I stepped on my horse and started back to camp.

We loose herded the horses on that good grass and water and the Yaquis were enjoying themselves when next day a little before dinner in rode Mr. Flustrated Rancher. He said that my horses were keeping his cattle from coming into that watering place and besides that they were eating up all the grass, and he believed if he was me, he would just push on out across the country. The forest ranger wouldn't ever do anything about it.

I said, "Mr. Rancher, you're messin' with my business right sharply. First you do me the favor of gettin' me stopped up in this nice country, then you decide you don't like the way me and the government is runnin' my business so you'll tell me how to change it. Now it may come as a right smart of a shock to you, but I've quit payin' you any mind and as long as my horses are doin' good and my men are restin', I'm not goin' to be interested in your suggestions about how me and the government timber man ought to run my business. It's about dinner time and we're fixin' to eat and since it's always been my practice to feed damn near any kind of a stray, it'll be all right if you want to stay for dinner."

He busted out in a batch of very unkind and unpolite bellerin' and rode off. And me and the Yaqui boys all had a big laugh while we ate a batch of beans, beef and taters.

I had begun to get a little restless and the Yaqui had been changing horses and just riding them around a little bit and changing them again for the want of something to do. We had a young bay mare in the bunch that was awful poor and I thought it was because she was shedding her teeth and couldn't graze very good, but the Yaqui had noticed her several times on the trail and they had diagnosed her among themselves as having the hollowtail. While they were doing nothing they said they ought to put the Indian treatment on that mare with the hollowtail but that was as far as it went.

Late in the afternoon of the third day, here come Mr. Forest Ranger. He had been instructed from somebody this side of Washington that there was no law against driving livestock in transit across a forest reservation. That word transit kind of throwed me, but he went on to explain that I was free to leave and he would suggest that I leave in the morning as soon as I could break camp and get away. I thanked him for the rest and hospitality and invited him to stay for supper. He didn't do that, but he stayed and drank some black coffee and then went back to running the government's forest business.

I knew that if we turned straight west like I had aimed to go to Peach Springs that I was liable to run into some more of these high tempered ranchers so I went up Chino Creek and rode into Seligman the next day a little before sundown and put my horses in the railroad stock pens. I found a place to buy some alfalfa for the horses, and the Indians and me went to a good chili joint so the horses and the Indians and me had a good night.

I had been knowing for a long time that I had drifted these horses too far north and that I wasn't going to have any horse business this late in the fall and should have shipped out toward home when I was at Tucson. From Tucson until now the trip was worthless so far as doing any horse business and I decided that when I got to a good shipping point, it was time to quit for the winter. But, we were pretty well settled in the stock pens and I thought it would be all right to stay a few days and see if there was any tradin' to be done before I moved on to Peach Springs.

The next day we brushed and curried horses and saddled and unsaddled and rode and worked all the young horses that we had been breaking along the way and even the other horses that hadn't been rode were gentle to work 'em all and catch. It was getting to where it turned pretty cold by late afternoon and the nights were real cold. I had plenty of bedroll and the Indians hadn't started complaining, but I think maybe some of them were probably a little cold. A little before dark they thought they should go uptown and look for some refreshment and excitement. They hadn't asked for any money before but they all wanted to draw a little now, and I let them have whatever they asked for provided it wasn't more than they had coming. They headed down to the wrong side of the railroad tracks to a bar and eatin' joint. I went back up to the other part of the town which wasn't too big and ate up a batch of grub, visited around a little and came back to camp and went to bed.

It was a moonlight night and crisp and cold. About eleven o'clock I heard a awful stir in my horses and was gettin' up when I heard the Yaquis doing lots of laughing and talking. I hollered at Chief and asked him what was going on. He kind of half climbed and half fell over the fence where the horses were and went to explaining to me with a tangled thick tongue that they had *mucho amigos* to help them put the Indian treatment on the hollowtail mare. He said, "We know you no care cause it make her better."

I had had some sleep so I layed and listened. There were seven or eight drunked-up, happy Indians catching this mustang mare and telling each other what to do. I decided I must be missing the show so I went ahead and got my clothes and looked over the fence about the time they were letting the mare up. She had bawled a little bit before they let her off the ground and was running around

the fence switching her tail, then laying down and wallering, getting up and then running again and making all kinds of maneuvers of trying to reach around with her mouth and bite her tail. Chief saw me watching through the fence. They were all laughing and talking and he ran over to me and said, "See, Indian medicine do horse much good."

I said, "Yeah, I see it does. It must be strong medicine," and asked, "Where did you put it and what is it?"

He said, "We split underside of tail and pour cut full of salt. This cure hollowtail and cause horse to have much go."

I said, "Yeah, I see. The same kind of treatment might work on an Indian. Suppose you get all this wild stuff tended to and get quiet and go to bed." Well, they staggered off over the fence with their friends instead of coming into camp.

The next morning a little after sunup, I was the only man in camp and cookin' breakfast when Chief came into camp. His face was swollen, his eyes red, his hands shaky, and he didn't waste any time amakin' some black coffee. When he had about the third cup down he said, "Other cowboys got much trouble."

I said, "Other cowboys! Looks like to me you got some too."

"Yeah," he said, "I got trouble too, but they in jail and sheriff sent me to tell you come bring money for fines."

I wasn't doing any good with my horses in town but I thought it would do my help good to stay in that jail about half a day to sober up and get remorseful instead of me havin' to put up with them during that time so I told Chief that maybe Indian belonged in jail. He said, "Maybe so, but they no like."

I said, "The Indians drew much money. Maybe they don't have enough comin' to pay their fines."

He said, "We work if you pay sheriff. You come go cause Chief got to go back to jail."

140

"Chief," I said, "you go back to jail. Maybe I'll come after awhile."

He said, "Oh, that don't do."

I had about finished eatin' my breakfast and said to Chief, "Why don't it do?"

"Jail no good for Indian."

Well, I made him go back to the sheriff and get put back in jail and I moseyed downtown and visited and about ten o'clock got to the jail. The Indians hadn't actually done anything bad, except get drunk and it was just kind of a way to help along the expenses in the sheriff's department, I think, but I paid their fines and told them to go and brush and clean off horses until I told them to stop. They sure didn't give me any back talk and headed for the stock pens. I had Tortilla fix a big dinner of beans and chili and flour tortillas and after they had eat up a batch of this grub and drank that granite pot of coffee empty about twice, I thought they were ready to handle horses.

We broke camp and packed and drifted west along the highway about ten miles before camping that night. This was a dry camp and in rather open country but it didn't make much difference since everything had been on water several days and we had started to drift soon after the middle of the day. The next night we camped close to some caves and near the town of Yavapai. The Indians were afraid of the caves and said that great spirits sometimes walked at night and I said, "Well, the spirits that you all had night before last ought to make you strong enough to not be afraid of these spirits."

They laughed and said it was different kind of spirits.

Next day we had some trouble along the highway with what few cars came by and that night drove the horses into the Santa Fe Railroad stock pens at Peach Springs.

141

Peach Springs was an old renowned shipping point for the Indian reservations and a few great big old ranches and there was generally plenty of stock cars on the tracks. There was a trading post and a general mercantile and very little else to the town and I could tell real quick that it wasn't going to be a good place to spend the winter because it was a long ways from feed and anything that I bought for the horses would have been shipped in and when it was snowed in entertainment would be however loud you could cuss by yourself.

It was too late in the fall for Indian trade and I decided it was time to ship out to a warmer climate but at the same time I didn't think I could sell these horses at home and make much money if I put a freight bill in them. I had left Marathon in November the year before and here I was in Peach Springs, Arizona, in November a year later. I had worked all year and spent most of the cash that I started out with and had lots of horses and nothing that I could do with 'em it seemed.

Owen Brothers were the biggest horse and mule dealers in the world and owned the auction markets at Kansas City, Memphis, Texarkana, and I'm sure other places that I didn't know about. They were a great breed of horse and mule traders — half Irish, half gypsy and if there were any government contracts or any other kind of horse business, Owen Brothers would either have the contract or be financing the men that did have 'em. Light-boned riding type of horses were plentiful and it looked like I might have gathered me a whole batch of nothin' in a year's time unless I could figure out somewhere to go with 'em.

One morning I went in the trading post and told the old man that I wanted to place a long distance telephone call, and I'd pay him for it when I got through talking or else I'd call collect. As I started to put in the call, I knew that Ferd Owen, the oldest one

142

and the brains of the outfit in Kansas City, knew me well and I had auctioneered for him in times past, and I thought he would take a collect call. In those days it wasn't unusual for it to take from an hour to half a day to make a long distance call that far away.

After I gave the operator the information and hung up to wait for her to call me back, I sat around the trading post figurin' on what I ought to tell him or ask him about these horses. I knew that if I started my conversation by saying, "Ferd, I've got a whole bunch of western mustangs," that he would suddenly know that he didn't have any market for them and he wouldn't know what he could do with them, but for me to go ahead and ship them to him and he would do the best he could. That would be the natural reaction of an old-time big operator in the horse and mule business, especially Ferd Owen.

I loafed around the trading post and eat up the candy and drank cokes and walked the floor about two hours, and the operator finally called back and said that Mr. Owen was on the line. He started out in a big friendly voice about how he hadn't seen or heard from me in a year or two and what was I doing in Arizona. After we got the formalities and niceties tended to I said, "Ferd, I hear by the grapevine that you're in need of a lot of light-boned pony horses on a government contract."

I was runnin' a bluff but if anybody had a government contract, horse and mule world generally knew about it. Ferd laughed right big and said, "That news gets way out yonder don't it."

I realized then that I wasn't runnin' a bluff and had actually tapped the old boy where it felt good. He said, "Ben, you already got 'em or do you want to buy 'em and callin' for a checkbook."

"Well, Ferd, I'm callin' for a checkbook whether I got 'em or I ain't got 'em."

It was the custom for Owen Brothers to stake nearly anybody

143

they knew to be a good buyer to go to the country and buy horses and mules with their checkbook and then they sold them to their best customers many times on credit and would be financing both ends of the operation sometimes running into the hundreds of thousands of dollars and in times past I had used his checkbook.

Ferd laughed about that and said, "I knew you'd want money one way or another."

I thought I had better get into what these horses might be worth and asked, "Ferd, what would some good, clean, young, broke to ride or broke to handle, from eight to nine hundred pound mares and geldings bring?"

He said, "Well, in Arizona I guess about $35 a head. That's liable to make 'em cost $50 in Kansas City and we've got a government contract to ship these horses to Cuba or they wouldn't be worth the freight."

I didn't want to shout over the telephone or laugh right out loud nor lose my breath but the thought of $35 a head was about to make me do all those things especially when I glanced out the window and there was a light snow falling.

I said, "You know I can't get many of that kind of horses without havin' to take some yearlings and twos and maybe some mares that are thin and unbroke."

He said, "If you take any of that kind, they're not worth much money and I'd want you to ship 'em to Hasse in Texarkana and send the good end of 'em to me here in Kansas City."

I asked, "And how about me drawin' some money when I load 'em?"

"Why, hell yes, that's all right. Just go to the bank and draw a draft on Owen Brothers if you ain't still got one of our checks in your pocket."

I said, "Well, I'm going to ship you four carloads of clean

144

young horses to Kansas City and one carload of gonnabe and has-beens to Texarkana, and the first bank I come to I'll draw a draft on you for a $1,000. After I'm back in Texas and settled for the winter, I'll let you know where to send me the rest of the money."

"Ben," he said, "you better get yourself ready for some of that four carloads not to pass government inspection and we'll pay you what they'll bring at auction and pay you the government price of $35 a head that we get past the inspector."

I said, " Ferd, Owen Brothers raised me to be used to a right smart of bushin' and some actually snide stealin' and tradin' on even a little bunch of horses and I know you can do a good job on a big bunch, so you ain't breakin' no news to me about the facts of life in the Owen Brothers horse and mule business."

He had a big laugh over that and said, "Go ahead and ship the stock and when you get to a bank, you can draw whatever money you want and when you get back home where you won't get robbed, let me know and I'll send you the rest of it."

And, then I told him, "This is the biggest and best horse trade I've made in over a year and this telephone call is costin' money and I've got my business tended to, so before you try to charge some of it back to my horses, I'd better say goodby and good luck and hang up."